Differentiating Instruction for At-Risk Students

What to Do and How to Do It

Rita Dunn and Andrea Honigsfeld

ROWMAN & LITTLEFIELD EDUCATION
Lanham • New York • Toronto • Plymouth, UK

Published in the United States of America
by Rowman & Littlefield Education
A Division of Rowman & Littlefield Publishers, Inc.
A wholly owned subsidiary of The Rowman & Littlefield Publishing Group, Inc.
4501 Forbes Boulevard, Suite 200, Lanham, Maryland 20706
www.rowmaneducation.com

Estover Road
Plymouth PL6 7PY
United Kingdom

British Library Cataloguing in Publication Information Available

Library of Congress Cataloging-in-Publication Data

Dunn, Rita Stafford, 1929-
Differentiating instruction for at-risk students : What to do and how to do it / Rita Dunn and Andrea Honigsfeld.
p. cm.
Includes bibliographical references.
ISBN-13: 978-1-57886-982-4 (cloth : alk. paper)
ISBN-10: 1-57886-982-X (cloth : alk. paper)
ISBN-13: 978-1-57886-983-1 (pbk. : alk. paper)
ISBN-10: 1-57886-983-8 (pbk. : alk. paper)
eISBN-13: 978-1-57886-984-8
eISBN-10: 1-57886-984-6
[etc.]
1. Effective teaching—United States. 2. Teacher-student relationships—United States. 3. Special education—United States. 4. Children with disabilities—Education—United States. 5. Children with social disabilities—Education—United States. 6. Learning disabled children—Education—United States. I. Honigsfeld, Andrea, 1965- II. Title.

LB1025.3.D86 2009
371.9—dc22 2008035429

∞™ The paper used in this publication meets the minimum requirements of American National Standard for Information Sciences—Permanence of Paper for Printed Library Materials, ANSI/NISO Z39.48-1992.
Manufactured in the United States of America.

This book is dedicated to all the
students and teachers with whom we have ever worked.

Contents

Preface: Why Do Many Children Struggle in School?

When given the chance to do so, parents report that their first two offspring are very different from each other and that the third born into the same family is unlike both older siblings. Parents also comment that whereas one child is relatively easy going, the other can be a problem at times.

Teachers see the same differences among same-age, same-grade students and agree that "in a perfect world" learners should be taught and treated as individuals. Teachers face the challenge of doing that with many different children in the same class. And although school administrators and government officials are very aware of the disparity between their educational beliefs and the daily practices they promote, they continue to require the identical behaviors and standardized achievement-test scores of all students in the same grade.

The extent of human differences in how individuals learn is mind-boggling and beyond the ken of most people. However, once we admit that different children require different ways of learning—but invariably are taught identically—it is easy to explain why so many struggle.

Some teachers think that they are responding to individual differences when they supplement lectures, readings, and discussions with computers, demonstrations, guests, hands-on projects, multimedia, small-group instruction, or trips. Those activities are no more effective than conventional teaching when provided across the board for everyone.

WHICH LEARNERS BECOME AT RISK?

Conventional teaching is effective for some, but devastating for more youth than you would believe! Ask any experienced teacher and they will describe children who do not learn conventionally.

1. Those living with single-parent, no-parent, homeless, impoverished, migrant, minority, or undereducated families;
2. Those whose parents are alcoholics, drug users, in prison, unemployed, or undereducated;
3. Those living in metropolitan or rural areas;
4. Those who do not speak English;
5. Those who cannot read in their own native language;
6. Boys more often than girls; and
7. Those who read poorly.

Teachers are unlikely to impact successfully on poverty and how children's parents behave, but we certainly can teach them to read well and to speak English fluently (Dunn & Blake, 2008; Dunn & DeBello, 1999).

WHAT CHALLENGES DO EDUCATORS FACE WHEN THEY TRY TO IMPROVE TEACHING?

The No Child Left Behind (NCLB) legislation mandated the improvement of student achievement and sought to measure gains through improved test scores. We urge you to consider the following eight major challenges we identified.

The first major challenge is that educators historically have sought to improve student achievement with data-driven decision making such as test scores, dropout rates, attendance numbers, opinion surveys, gap analyses, demographic statistics, and performance growth. There is no way that teachers can use such data to identify underlying causes of students' learning problems or to improve instruction. Such data do not reveal the *causes* of students' learning problems, and they certainly do not suggest how to improve instruction. Such data only tell us what is wrong—not *why*, and certainly not *how to replace what is wrong with what is right.*

The second challenge is that many educators latch on to every commercially well-packaged new program that comes along, without first methodically researching with whom it worked and with whom it did not. Many administrators admire new ideas, but accept without question their commercial promoters' statements concerning the effectiveness of their merchandise.

The third challenge is that teachers and administrators are required to adopt new fads on face value. It is only after implementation that the profession finds that the new program works no better than the old discarded one—but perhaps with different students.

The fourth challenge is that teachers often are required to implement more than one new program at a time. Adopting a new instructional program requires sober diligence, experimentation to determine for whom it works and for whom it does not, and knowledge of how to conduct research objectively.

That leads to the fifth challenge—teachers do not have evaluation skills to determine the effects of the instruction they deliver. And when more than one approach is explored or instituted simultaneously, no one actually knows what achievement gains—or decreases—were contributed by which.

The sixth challenge is that commercial vendors and consultants use the word *research* differently from the way it is used by professional researchers. Only experimental research that examines the effects of each program on students' achievement, attitudes, or behaviors provides valuable knowledge concerning whether it is worthy of adoption or not.

The seventh challenge is that many researchers insist on an experimental/control design, believing that it alone provides objective data. That is an inaccurate perception when we are seeking to respond to *individual* strengths and weaknesses. Those who successfully have been involved in school-based studies realize that a counterbalanced and repeated-measures design is a much stronger plan for identifying which method is best for Sally as opposed to which is best for Steven. Because we know that individuals learn differently from members of their own family, as well as from their classmates, seeking *group* improvement is not as efficient or promising as identifying what helps each at-risk student improve significantly.

The eighth challenge is that "at-risk" students do not all learn the same way. There is no single approach that will improve achievement for all and, therefore, there is no best way to teach all children to read. Those who still think there is only reveal their limited understanding of well-controlled research. There are many good ways to conduct research, but the only way we can be certain of which approach is best for Sally—or Steven—is to try every approach with each child and see which produces the most learning, the most retention, and the best attitudes toward learning.

WHY THE APPROACH PRESENTED IN THIS BOOK HAS IT ALL

We have worked backward. We started with four decades of research to determine which methods worked best with which children. Through that approach, we learned what worked best with auditory versus visual/print versus visual/picture versus tactual, versus kinesthetic learners. Through research, we learned that some people only can listen to someone speak while the listener verbally interacts—either with the speaker, or someone close by, or with herself. We learned who learns best independently without others nearby, who learns best in a pair or in a small group, and who needs a teacher. We also learned who needs an authoritative teacher and who performs best with a collegial teacher.

We learned who needs quiet and who needs sound while concentrating, and who is distracted by either or both; who needs bright light and who becomes hyperactive in the very same illumination. We learned who learns best passively and who requires active engagement; who thinks sequentially and who thinks globally—and how to teach to both types of processors simultaneously. We learned about students at every age who need high structure and those who defy imposed structure of almost any kind. We also learned who tends to do exactly as their teachers ask, and who will not.

In addition to all that, we have experimented with seven different ways of teaching an identical curriculum and discovered for whom each works well and for whom it does not. All of this is in this book and will guide any willing teacher to reduce the number of at-risk students in the class, the school, and the district. All the research verification available is on our website accessible to all (www.learningstyles.net). Read this book, read the documentation on our website, and then follow these easy-to-implement, step-by-step guidelines. At-risk students have no one else to rescue them. You and we are their only hope.

Rita Dunn and Andrea Honigsfeld

Acknowledgments

The authors extend a special note of appreciation to Joann-Marie Gamble, Rickey G. Moroney, Lucia Posillico, and Susan Rundle for their assistance with Adobe Photoshop and Adobe Illustrator and Shannon Kelly Kane for her help with formatting illustrations.

We also would like to acknowledge all those who contributed photographs or examples of learning-style implementation from their own practice to this book: Rosette Allegretti, Sabahat Basusta, Roger Bloom, Maria Dove, Jennifer Ecuyer, Dr. Lois Favre, Dr. Tone Guldahl, Charlotte Humphrey, Dr. Rahmah Jadid Pengiran Jadid, Dr. Angela Klavas, Susan Rundle, Kaan Sagnak, Eileen Ward, and Roz Alia Zin.

Gratitude also is extended to our families for their support throughout this wonderful journey—Dr. Kenneth John Dunn and Howard, Benjamin, and Jacob Honigsfeld!

Last but not least we would like thank the staff at Rowman & Littlefield who supported this project from the very beginning and helped turn it into an outstanding publication—Dr. Thomas Koerner, vice president and editorial director, Melissa McNitt, associate editor, and Maera Winters, editorial assistant to Dr. Koerner.

Chapter One

Who Are Students at Risk of Academic Failure and How Should We Teach Them?

Educational theories? Plenty with which to align ourselves! Educational innovations? Too many to keep track of! Instructional techniques? Dozens from which to choose! Quick fixes and fads? Sure!

Why then are we still struggling to meet the needs of at-risk students in almost every classroom? Schools and school districts across the world seem to be spending fortunes on well-publicized strategies—and there is always the latest bandwagon! We remember Constructivism taking over from Direct Teaching, Cooperative Learning perceived as the answer to individual failure, and Multiple Intelligences debunking the IQ myth! The 1990s were dubbed as *The Decade of the Brain* and of course Brain-Based Learning flooded our schools. There is no shortage of approaches that respond to seemingly ongoing education crises. And now we're seeking to aid autistic children.

Standards promote authentic, active learning experiences, and the latest buzzword term, *response to intervention*, proposes a three-tier system to alleviate struggling students' inability to meet the requirements of the No Child Left Behind legislation. What is common among all these approaches and the dozens not mentioned here is that they claim they will turn education around.

Despite districts' investments in heavy financial and personnel resources, conventional teaching—lectures, discussions, readings, and repeated paper-and-pencil tests—often continues to dominate classrooms internationally. This is particularly accurate at the secondary level. Unfortunately, despite the plethora of approaches adopted, the number of at-risk students seems to be growing.

WHO ARE TYPICALLY RECOGNIZED AS BEING AT RISK?

Officially classified at-risk students come in various categories that include each of the following groups. Students who:

- are diagnosed (or misdiagnosed) as learning disabled;
- grow up in isolated communities and do not begin learning English until they enter school;
- do not speak the language because they recently arrived from another country;
- live in poverty and lack basic educational resources in their homes;
- are the children of migrant workers or undocumented immigrants whose presence in our schools is transient; and
- are homeless and do not have their basic needs of safety and security met.

Now consider this. There are many more students who are at risk but do not fit into any of these well-known categories. At first, they seem to be doing well in school; then they start falling behind, become chronic underachievers, and fail to learn to read. Finally they become restless or hyperactive. Most of the youth in this category are those who:

- process new and difficult information globally and have a rough time following analytic, step-by-step teaching;
- sing or talk to themselves when they should be concentrating;
- wear caps or visors in school despite rules to the contrary;
- cannot sit still;
- constantly fidget and are easily distracted;
- frequently "play" with hand-held items;
- don't seem to "try" or take school seriously;
- have a short attention span;
- are nonconforming or disobedient;
- apparently "walk to the tune of a different drummer";
- are peer rather then teacher oriented;
- seem bored;
- cannot concentrate or pay attention to the teacher's oral directions or lectures for more than a few minutes;
- may read, but cannot remember what they read;
- draw or doodle while listening;
- refuse to remain in their seats;
- appear tired or listless when they should be alert;

- surreptitiously nibble or snack in class; and
- usually can't answer their teacher's questions.

These youth live in every community and attend every school, whether their native country is Australia, Brunei, Bermuda, Denmark, Finland, Norway, the Philippines, Singapore, Sweden, or the United States. They are in every institution, regardless of whether it is in an affluent, middle-class, or poor neighborhood. Learning style does not discriminate by ethnicity, race, or socioeconomic status. However, it does discriminate by achievement level, gender, and brain processing.

WHY DO STUDENTS BECOME AT RISK?

Most of our middle schools and high schools still follow the industrial model of utilizing *cells and bells*. Each classroom functions in isolation on a strict 42-minute schedule. All learning must to be completed in exactly the same amount of time. No wonder *chalk-and-talk*, question-and-answer periods, and quickly administered written quizzes dominate instruction.

High-stakes testing makes the situation worse. No matter how much teachers have tried to elevate struggling students' achievement, certain youth do not measure up to school, state, or federal standards. Then educators incorrectly label them "at risk," "special needs," "special education," or "learning disabled," and society as a whole has accepted these imposed designations. Researchers have shown that these children can and do learn when they are taught with instructional strategies and resources responsive to their individual learning styles—and they do so in the same amount of time as *average* learners. Therefore, it is our perception that most of these learners are not learning disabled; rather, they are *teaching disabled*.

THE MILLENNIAL STUDENT

Simplicio (2007) described 21st-century students, or *millennial students*, as those who attend better-equipped schools with ample resources and classes that are taught by well-qualified teachers. Although this may be accurate for some, he cautiously acknowledged that "although millennial students are better informed, more technologically savvy, and worldlier, they are also more diverse, more demanding, needier, and harder to teach than any other students in the past" (p. 2). Teachers throughout the world have seen demographic changes and technological advancements that efficiently provide many youth with cell phones, BlackBerries, laptops, iPods, sidekicks, and so on! Teachers have witnessed their pupils' increasing dependence, on the one hand, and their expanding autonomy on the other. Teachers have observed the decline of parental and school authority and the extension of students' *rights* beyond what was previously considered appropriate decision making for adolescents.

WHAT THIS BOOK CAN HELP ACCOMPLISH

We will explain how to reverse student failure by describing how to teach to students' learning styles in gradual, easy-to-implement, cost-effective steps. We will address the following key issues:

1. what *learning style* really is;
2. what sets the Dunn and Dunn Learning-Styles Model apart from all other learning-style models;
3. the primary instructional needs of students who are unable to concentrate on, process, internalize, and retain new and difficult information;
4. how educators can respond to the diverse needs of students at all grade levels and in all content areas to effectively reverse underachievement;
5. the extensive research supporting the Dunn and Dunn Learning-Styles Model; and
6. how teachers can integrate learning-style-responsive approaches into their class, school, district, and state, federal, or ministry curriculum requirements.

We have worked with thousands of teachers. Some were novices, others seasoned; some were skeptics, others never doubted the success they would have with learning styles. But all needed to know the research demonstrating that learning-styles-based instruction really works. They needed to be shown how to find the time to incorporate new strategies when their plates were already full and overflowing. Another concern was what to do when the supervisor mandates a different instructional construct or if you are the only one in your building trying to use learning styles.

We acknowledge that it is no small feat to help at-risk students in any school, whether they are classified that way because of external circumstances or inappropriate instruction. However, not teaching to each child's unique learning style is a disservice to that youngster, to the school, and to the larger educational community. We invite our readers—whether new to the field of education or experienced, whether true skeptics or open to new ideas, whether confident that they know how to reach at-risk youth or desperate for something—anything—that works, to allow us to *teach* rather than merely tell about learning styles. We will explain and illustrate every point we make concerning at-risk students and, through our approaches, readers will learn how to eliminate that category in their classes—as many others have done (Dunn & DeBello, 1999; also see www.learningstyles.net).

REFLECTION POINTS

1. Consider the teaching challenges you have faced in your classroom. With which interventions have you experimented? What were the outcomes?
2. Analyze the sociopolitical, economical, and technological context in which many of today's students grow up compared with when you were a student. What are the most prevalent similarities and differences?

Chapter Two

What Is Learning Style?

Although diverse theorists have contributed to an understanding of how learning generally occurs, Dunn and Dunn (1972, 1978, 1992, 1993, 1999) have engaged in ongoing experimental studies to assess the effects of their model's variables on kindergarten-through-adult students' achievement. Without extensive experimentation, it is impossible to document what makes the identical instructional strategy effective for some learners and ineffective for others. That specific lack of experimental research originally led Ebel (1969) to conclude that until 1969 little progress had been made "toward bridging the gap between laboratory psychology and the study of school learning" (p. 726). However, during the four decades since Ebel's observation, at least 850 investigations were undertaken by researchers at more than 135 different institutions of higher education to determine exactly what educators need to know about learning and teaching (see www.learningstyles.net).

It has taken years of experimental studies to recognize and acknowledge the many errors that we teachers at all educational levels make on a daily basis as we try to teach an entire class with a single approach to any subject—particularly grammar, foreign language, mathematics, reading, or vocabulary. There is no *best* way to teach any content. There are only good, poor, better, and alternative ways of teaching each individual. From extensive research, we have learned the value of identifying and responding to each individual's learning-style *strengths* (Dunn & Griggs, 2007a).

HOW DO LEARNING-STYLE MODELS VARY?

In view of the many learning-style models that have emerged since the 1970s and the confusion that even the Middle States Commission on Higher

Education (2003) admitted concerning them, it makes sense to compare how the models are similar to and different from each other. More than a quarter of a century ago, Dunn, DeBello, Brennan, Krimsky, and Murrain (1981) reported that, despite varied terminology, eight major theorists in the United States shared very similar perceptions of what constituted an individual's *learning style*.

For example, motivation and different sociological preferences were addressed by Canfield and Lafferty (1976), Dunn and Dunn (1972), Gregorc (1982, 1985), Hill (1971), and Ramirez and Castaneda (1974). Structure was included in the learning-style descriptors of Canfield and Lafferty, Dunn and Dunn (1992, 1993, 1999), Gregorc, Hill, Hunt, and Ramirez and Castaneda.

Consideration of Perceptual Modalities

One interesting difference among the models is that, with the single exception of Ramirez and Castaneda, each of these aforementioned theorists and Kolb (1976) categorized perception as a learning style, rather than a brain-processing style. Conversely, the National Association of Secondary School Principals' (NASSP) Model (Keefe, Languis, Letteri, & Dunn 1985) was based on an information-processing construct and incorporated perception into brain processing. Indeed, dimensions of brain processing were part of many models, such as those of Canfield and Lafferty (1976), Dunn and Dunn, (1972–2005), Gregorc (1982), Hill (1971), Kolb (1976), Ramirez and Castaneda (1974), and Schmeck (1977). On the other hand, the basic cornerstone of McCarthy's (1990), Gregorc's, and Kolb's learning-style models stemmed from Jung's focus on personality as depicted in the Myers-Briggs Type Indicator (Lawrence, 1982).

Consideration of Goal Setting and Instructional Environments

Other important differences separated these models. For example, Canfield and Lafferty (1976) were the only ones to address goal setting. The Dunns (1972) were the first to describe an individual's ability to concentrate better or less well in alternative instructional environments dependent upon the availability of:

- bright versus soft illumination;
- formal versus informal seating;
- opportunities for mobility versus continuing passivity;
- sound (music or conversation) versus quiet; and
- cool versus warm temperatures.

Although the value of environmental variations is internationally recognized today (Boström & Kroksmark, 2005; Brunner & Dunn, 1997; Buli-Holmberg, Guldahl, & Jensen, 2007; Calissendorff, 2006; DiSebastian, 1994; Dunn & Brunner, 1997; Orden & Ramos, 2005; Pengiran-Jadid, 1998), four decades ago there was virtually no research on learners' preferences for these variables or intake (snacking) when focusing on new and difficult academic information.

In addition to recognizing that some individuals focus in different sociological patterns, the Dunns differentiated among learning alone, in pairs, as part of a team, with peers, with a collegial versus an authoritative adult, and in a variety of approaches rather than in patterns and routines (Dunn & Dunn, 1972).

Consideration of Culture, Study Skills, and Strengths

Well in advance of society's concerns with multiculturalism and diversity, both Hill's and Ramirez and Castaneda's models included culture as a crucial aspect of learning style. Then, as recently as 2007, Buli-Holmberg et al. reflected on how the Dunns' learning-style model was perceived in Scandinavia as opposed to in other parts of the world.

As early as the mid-1980s, NASSP released its secondary model that essentially paralleled the Dunns' 21 elements, but also included study skills. Thus, NASSP's *Learning Style Profile* referenced study skills as a learning style, whereas the Dunns' books (1972, 1978, 1992, 1993, 1999) described a variety of study skills that they perceived as being more or less responsive to students who learned in patterns extremely different from those of same-age classmates based on unique environmental, emotional, sociological, physiological, and psychological learning-style preferences.

Consideration of Brain Processing

In contrast with the Dunns' position that both global and analytic predispositions each become a strength when students are taught in ways that respond to their particular style (Dunn & Dunn, 1993, p. 40), the NASSP Learning Style Profile (LSP) identified brain processing as either high or low *analytic*—intimating that analytic was the benchmark for intelligence. However, prior to development of the NASSP model, several researchers had reported that when analytics were taught analytically and globals were taught globally, each achieved significantly better test scores than when they were taught with dissonant strategies (Brennan, 1984; Douglas, 1979; Trautman, 1979). Later, Orazio (1999) and Sagan (2002) both showed that, except for approximately

12%–15% of their extremely analytic, middle-school students, the majority of global learners mastered mathematics better—and enjoyed learning it more—with anecdotes, tactual and kinesthetic game-like resources, and stories in an informal classroom environment than traditionally in conventional classrooms. In contrast, their analytic counterparts preferred learning conventionally.

Unfortunately, global students taught analytically *become* our low achievers. As distressing as that realization is, low achievement has been reversed when instruction was altered to respond to poorly achieving students' learning styles at the elementary (Andrews, 1990; Braio, Beasley, Dunn, Quinn, & Buchanan, 1997; Favre, 2003; Klavas, 1991; Klavas, Dunn, Griggs, Gemake, Geisert, & Zenhausern, 1994), middle (Cody, 1983; Crossley, 2007; Elliot, 1991; Fine, 2002, 2003; Jarsonbeck, 1984; Quinn, 1999), secondary (Brunner & Majewski, 1990; Mitchell, Dunn, Klavas, Lynch, Montgomery, Murray, 2002), and college (Dunn, Bruno, Sklar, Zenhausern, & Beaudry, 1990; Lenehan, Dunn, Ingham, Murray, & Signer, 1994) levels in school systems across the United States (Dunn & DeBello, 1999).

Consideration of Bipolar versus Comprehensive Models

DeBello (1990) described some models, such as Gregorc's (1982), Hunt's (1982), Kolb's (1976), and McCarthy's (1990) as being narrow in focus because they addressed only one or two variables on a bipolar continuum. He perceived the Dunn and Dunn, Hill, and NASSP models as *comprehensive* because each required analyses of many variables. DeBello also perceived the Myers-Briggs Type Indicator (Lawrence, 1982) as a *personality index* rather than a learning-style identifier. Too, DeBello (1990) and Tendy and Geiser (1998–1999) analyzed McCarthy's 4 MAT System as being a *lesson-plan* that prescribed teaching all students in the same class with identical resources, in the same sequence, at the same time, and in the same amount of time. Those three reviewers reported that the quality of learning-styles research varied from model to model and from study to study.

Learning-style theorists recognize that individuals' cognitive, affective, physiological, sociological, and psychological patterns contribute to their academic outcomes. According to Keefe (1982), the NASSP former director of research, those patterns serve as relatively stable "indicators of how learners perceive, interact with, and respond to the learning environment" (p. 4). Apparently, the complex nature of learning style requires a multidimensional model to reflect the many individual differences resulting from each person's biological, developmental, and psychological experiences.

Each learning-style model has been evaluated extensively (Curry, 1987; DeBello, 1990; Dunn et al., 1981; Tendy & Geiser, 1998–1999). Gradually, researchers' foci shifted from identification of specific *best* strategies for all similarly aged learners to identification of strategies responsive to students with specific characteristics when they are confronted with challenging academic tasks.

A COMPREHENSIVE APPROACH TO LEARNING STYLES

According to Dunn and Dunn (1972, 1975, 1978, 1992, 1993, 1999), learning style is the way each student begins to concentrate on, process, internalize, and remember new and difficult academic information. People can learn material that is easy for them in the *wrong* style; few can master challenging academic material unless it is learned through their strengths. Restak (1979) and Thies (1979) both theorized that learning style is comprised of a combination of biological and developmental characteristics that make the identical instructional environments, methods, and resources effective for some learners and ineffective for others. Most people have learning-style *preferences*, but individuals' preferences differ significantly. The stronger the preference, the more important it is to provide compatible instructional strategies (Braio et al., 1997; Crossley, 2007; Favre, 2003; Fine, 2002, 2003).

Most teachers can learn to teach to diverse learning styles and most upper-elementary and middle school students can be taught to capitalize on their learning-style strengths. The less academically successful students are in traditional classrooms, the more crucial it is for their teachers to accommodate their learning-style preferences (Dunn & DeBello, 1999).

THE DUNN AND DUNN LEARNING-STYLES MODEL

Rita and Ken Dunn describe learning style as individuals' reactions to each of 21 elements when concentrating on new and difficult academic knowledge or skills. To capitalize on their natural strengths, students need to be made aware of their:

- personal reactions to their immediate instructional environment—sound versus silence, bright versus soft lighting, warm versus cool temperatures, and formal versus informal seating;

- own emotionality—motivation, persistence, responsibility (conformity versus nonconformity), and preferences for externally imposed structure versus personal options;
- sociological preferences for learning alone, with peers, with either a collegial or authoritative adult, and/or in a variety of ways as opposed to in patterns or routines;
- physiological characteristics—perceptual strengths (auditory, visual-text versus visual picture, tactual, kinesthetic, and/or verbal/kinesthetic inclinations), time-of-day energy levels, intake (snacking versus no nibbling while concentrating), and/or mobility versus passivity needs; and
- global versus analytic processing (Dunn, Cavanaugh, Eberle, & Zenhausern, 1982; Dunn, Bruno et al., 1990; Guastello & Burke, 1998–1999). (See figure 2.1)

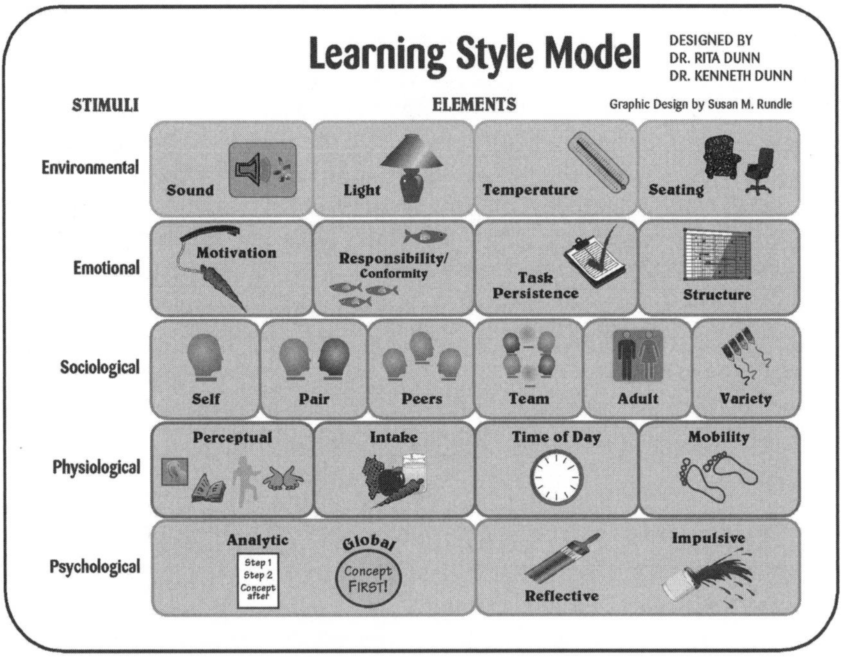

Figure 2.1. Dunn and Dunn Learning-Styles Model

HOW TO IDENTIFY STUDENTS' LEARNING STYLES

Teachers intuitively know that each child learns differently from the next. Sometimes they are able to observe those differences in their students' behaviors during in-school instructional time. More often those learning-style traits either are not apparent or are misinterpreted. Why does a pupil fidget? Is he disinterested in the material or is he a tactual learner who needs to manipulate objects while learning? Does he need mobility and is he unable to concentrate while sitting passively? Is he global and unable to focus on fact after fact without an understanding of how that information affects him personally?

To identify how a child learns, we recommend that you use one of the following learning-style assessment tools. Each instrument has been developed to address a particular age group. Each has been field tested both nationally and internationally to establish its validity and reliability. Translations are available in selected other languages (see www.learningstyles.net).

1. Elementary Learning Style Assessment (ELSA)
   ELSA (Dunn, Rundle, & Burke, 2007) is designed for children ages 7–9. ELSA includes three stories, each followed by a series of questions that assess students' individual learning styles. Before they begin, users are prompted to choose a story either about pirates or the circus. Humor, illustrations, and exciting story elements make the instrument interesting to youngsters who are made aware that there are no *right* or *wrong* answers to the questions posed.
2. Learning Style: The Clue to You! (LS:CY!)
   LS:CY (Dunn & Burke, 1998) is appropriate for ages 9–13. Similar to ELSA, the assessment of learning style occurs through a global format. Students read a detective story as they answer questions about their own learning inclinations.
3. Learning in Vogue: Elements of Style (LIVES)
   LIVES (Dunn & Missere, 2007) is designed for ages 14–18. An opening poem invites students to consider styles that are fashionable. Stories, humor, and illustrations help high school students determine their personal learning styles.

Each instrument identifies an individual's learning patterns—also considered learning *strengths*. Each analysis of style summarizes the environmental, emotional, sociological, physiological, and psychological inclinations that each student has for learning. After taking any of the above assessments, students can print a one-page profile of their learning-style preferences, as well as a detailed report that interprets the results. Students also receive practical ideas for using their personal style to understand and remember new and difficult information.

Assessing students' learning styles is the first step toward differentiating instruction based on students' existing strengths rather than their weaknesses.

At-risk students need to recognize their strengths, and so must all teachers who work with them throughout the day. Teachers must teach students to express their learning preferences verbally, allow students to advocate for strategies responsive to their personal learning needs, and invite parents to information meetings so they better understand their daughter's or son's learning style and the approach being introduced to address those needs.

Use the information in Textbox 2.1 to design a step-by-step implementation plan. The three-stage process is presented incrementally at the end of each chapter. We now are entering Stage 1! Although you may skip one or more stages along the way, you need to identify each at-risk student's learning style or you cannot credibly differentiate instruction in any logical fashion and anticipate that these youngsters will reveal measurable improvement on standardized achievement tests.

Textbox 2.1. How to Get Started with the Learning-Styles Implementation Process

STAGE 1

Learning-Styles Assessment
(See www.learningstyles.net for LS assessment tools)

- Share information with students, parents, all teachers.
- Help students use LS profile and study guide to become self-directed learners.

Designed by Angela Klavas, Ed.D. Adapted with permission from "Learning-Style Process of Implementation with the Dunn and Dunn Model" (Dunn and Dunn, 1993, p. 449).

TO WHAT EXTENT DOES LEARNING STYLE INFLUENCE INDIVIDUALS?

No one is impacted by all the variables in any model. Some children are affected by certain elements and others by different elements. Thus, when using only a one- or two-dimensional model, the very variables that might produce the most achievement gain for one youngster could be the very ones *not* included in that construct. Therefore, we chose the above multidimensional model as the basis for describing how to reach and teach at-risk students because it is comprehensive, has been well researched with many different achievement, age, and at-risk groups, and provides practitioner-oriented instructional treatments for improving student achievement and attitudes toward learning. See chapters 3 through 11 for practical approaches to implementing the Dunn and Dunn Learning-Styles Model in its complexity, chapter 12 for the research behind this model, and chapter 13 for legal implications for responding to individuals' styles.

REFLECTION POINTS

1. Why is it important to use a comprehensive model to identify individual differences?
2. Why do you believe different models emphasize different variables?

Chapter Three

Teaching Global Students Globally

Mrs. Blake introduced the concept of a global economy to her fourth graders *globally*. Read what she said and see if you can figure out what was *global* about how she introduced this topic.

> When my friends and I were your age, we talked about what we would do to earn a living and where we would work. Some of us only finished high school and got jobs in the neighborhood working in local businesses and stores. Others went to college and became accountants, nurses, social workers, or teachers. Those friends got jobs in different parts of our city. Others went to graduate school and became doctors, engineers, or lawyers. Those friends established practices in many different places—wherever young practitioners could get a start. Some opened an office in the neighborhood, others in small towns upstate. Some moved to other states. Three became physicists or scientists and worked at the Centers for Disease Control in Atlanta, Georgia. Some were very talented in art, dance, or music. Those relocated in urban centers like Boston, Hollywood, or New York, where there was work available in the arts. One moved to Washington, D. C., to work for a senator.
>
> When my own children grew up, their dreams led them to other parts of the world. One of my sons joined a theater group and traveled throughout the United States and Europe. Another was sent to Singapore to build the first international video cable computer system for a large financial firm called Morgan Stanley. Another represented his firm in Tokyo and London.
>
> *Your* children—and maybe *you*—will think nothing of living in Argentina, Brazil, China, France, Germany, India, or Turkey. Why? Because those nations are where jobs will be for people who live in a *global* economy! You need to understand what a global economy is, because that is the world we are living in right now, and before we realize it, *you* will want to earn a living and will need

to consider where the best opportunities lie! Frankly, I wouldn't be surprised if one day some of you were working in space!

People often are analytic, global, or integrated. Most analytics want detailed information and think in step-by-step sequences. That is how many teachers teach because that is how they were taught when they were young. And of course, that is how they plan and teach each lesson.

Given that many teachers teach analytically, you can imagine how surprised we were to learn that more school-age children are *global*—the opposite of being analytic. It is important to understand that a majority of teachers teach analytically and that most students are global because *the closer the match between how a student learns and how a teacher teaches, the higher the student's grade point average* (Cafferty, 1980).

Almost three decades ago, researchers began noting that global and analytic students concentrate in very different ways (Dunn, Bruno, et al., 1990; Dunn, Cavanaugh, et al., 1982; Sagan, 2002). Furthermore, when globals are taught analytically, they achieve significantly *less well* than when they are taught globally. They also perform less well on analytic tests—those that ask specific questions and require precise, correct answers. However, when the attitudes of global versus analytic processors are examined about learning and testing, the extremes in both groups strongly prefer approaches that complement their own brain-processing styles.

CHARACTERISTICS OF GLOBAL PROCESSORS

When global processors have to master challenging academic content, they generally:

- need to see how that information relates to them and their lives before they actually begin focusing on it;
- work nicely in small-groups;
- read for overall ideas, skip details, understand items in context, read "between the lines," intuit understandings, and skim passages;
- relate what they learn to their personal experiences and the people they know;
- enjoy stories about others' lives to make *connections*;
- see relationships and like analogies;

- work on different tasks simultaneously; they "multitask,"
- can ignore other things happening *while* they are learning;
- often answer questions with, "It depends" or "Sometimes I do and sometimes I don't;" and
- prefer summaries rather than lengthy explanations.

Every global does not exhibit all these traits, but most have many of them.

CHARACTERISTICS OF ANALYTIC PROCESSORS

Conversely, analytics tend to:

- learn in an ordered sequence (step-by-step; what came first, what followed, and then what followed that);
- analyze a problem and then reach a decision based on information;
- be interested in and often remember details;
- concentrate best either alone or in a pair rather than in a group;
- be disinterested in the personal experiences of others;
- do one thing at a time and be easily distracted when concentrating;
- dislike vague question forms such as, "Just suppose . . ." or "Imagine if . . .";
- prefer specific grading criteria and feedback; and
- prefer outlines, templates, and representative models.

ANALYTIC VERSUS GLOBAL ENVIRONMENTAL PREFERENCES WHEN LEARNING

Strangely, these two types of processors concentrate in different settings. For example, analytics often tend to need quiet, bright light, formal seating, and little or no intake *while* concentrating. They eat or snack *after* they have completed their tasks and tend to work on a single assignment until it is completed. Conversely, global students often concentrate best with background music or conversation, low illumination, and informal seating—such as a lounge chair, couch, bed, or carpeting. They take several breaks as they work and often engage in more than one task at the same time. Too, globals often eat, drink, chew, or smoke while thinking (Dunn, Bruno, et al., 1990; Dunn, Cavanaugh, et al., 1982; Sagan, 2002).

Guidelines for Teaching Analytic Students

Because analytic students often function well with traditional teaching, many of the following suggestions tend to meet their instructional needs.

1. Write key words on the board, transparencies, or slides.
2. Provide oral and visual explanations.
3. Answer questions in detail.
4. Alert them to printed directions, objectives, and test dates.
5. Proceed step-by-step through required information.
6. Underline or highlight important facts on handouts.
7. Use question-and-answer segments.
8. Test periodically and provide feedback on details and sequence.

Guidelines for Teaching Global Students

Because global students often do not function well with traditional teaching, many of the following suggestions tend to meet their instructional needs.

1. Introduce lessons globally—with an anecdote, cartoon, drama, joke, or story.
2. Relate your introduction to the concept or information you want them to learn.
3. Provide an overview of the topic and a sense of purpose for mastering the material or skill.
4. Include opportunities for them to discover some information on their own and to share it creatively by making an instructional resource to teach someone else the information.
5. Provide small-group experiences such as Team Learning, Circle of Knowledge, Group Analysis, or Brainstorming (see chapter 7).
6. Relate facts to a central theme or story and to experiences that are known to these learners.
7. Provide many types of instructional materials, particularly tactual resources such as Electroboards, Flip Chutes, and Task Cards (see chapter 5).
8. Provide kinesthetic experiences such as acting, puppetry, role playing, and Floor Games (see chapter 6).
9. Provide frequent feedback as questions arise.

WHEN YOU WANT TO TEACH GLOBAL AND ANALYTIC STUDENTS AT THE SAME TIME

Because the two groups begin concentrating differently, when you know that you have some of both in your class, experiment with the following.

1. Introduce each new topic or lesson globally—with a *short* anecdote, cartoon, drama, joke, or story.
2. Assign global learners a Team Learning with inference questions *first*, followed by factual questions, and then by creative applications—in that order. At the same time, assign analytic learners the same Team Learning but with the factual questions first, followed by the inference questions, and then by the creative applications—in that order. The questions may be identical, but their sequencing should differ.
3. Give both groups homework that requires a creative application of the knowledge emphasized in the Team Learning. Therefore, each student, or pair of students, should have to *make* something that teaches the same information in a novel way, such as through an Electroboard, crossword puzzle, Flip Chute, Floor Game, Pic-A-Hole, poem, rap, set of Task Cards, a video, and so forth. In the creative application required in the Team Learning, children are developing their responses in a group. However, in the homework applications, they develop their project independently or in a pair.
4. Allow/encourage students to share each other's creative projects to reinforce the information again in a novel way and to correct any existing errors.
5. Display/mount the students' creative projects and allow time to examine, share, and use them.
6. Use a Circle of Knowledge to review the most important facts in the Team Learning (see chapter 7).
7. Use a Group Analysis to promote creative thinking and give impulsives a chance to shine (see chapter 7).
8. Review the information in a game-like teamed competition.
9. Administer a test on the same information.
10. Compare global students' test scores when taught globally in contrast with when they are taught analytically.
11. Share the results with the students.

SAMPLE GLOBAL ACTIVITIES DESIGNED FOR AT-RISK STUDENTS

The following examples from teachers whose classrooms we visited illustrate their efforts to introduce lessons globally. They used anecdotes, drama, puppetry, and stories to offer visual input through realia (authentic objects used for instructional purposes), artwork, and pictures.

In a second-grade class, the teacher is about to start a new science unit on the life cycle of the butterfly. Instead of sequentially explaining the stages (from egg, larva, pupa, to butterfly), she pulls out a colorful, plush butterfly puppet from behind her back and dramatically tells a story about its life before becoming a butterfly.

A fourth-grade class embarks on a unit on the rock cycle with one of the children's parents describing her experiences while hiking on a dormant volcano in Iceland. She includes a brief slide show and tells about the unusual local practice of baking bread in a hole dug into the side of the still-warm volcano!

In a sixth-grade English lesson on Greek mythology, a few boys and girls have been coached to introduce this topic by dramatizing several legends that the class will be required to read. The purpose of this activity is to have classmates guess the themes of the stories before they have been formally introduced. One boy repeatedly pushes a gigantic beach ball up a makeshift slope, only to watch it roll back down again (the legend of Sisyphus). A girl opens a huge appliance box and pulls out a dark scarf, a flower, and a plastic skeleton. She then seems horrified and desperately tries to resist other items from emerging from the box while simultaneously pushing these things back into it (Pandora's box).

The teacher of a seventh-grade class studying the Civil War brings in some of his grandfather's treasured collection and tells the story behind a bullet, a coin, and a yellowed prayer book. Every student's eyes are on him as he holds up each item and shares a true story (or anecdote) about these memorabilia.

In another social studies class studying World War II, the teacher introduces the U.S. internment camps in which all people of Japanese descent were housed between 1942 and 1945. She decides against mandating the reading of the highly acclaimed, award-winning picture book, *Baseball Saved Us* by Mochizuki (1995) because she prefers permitting the students' options from among several alternatives. However, she projects the book's scanned artwork onto the screen as she describes how Japanese-American boys often spent their days, weeks, and months in the Arizona desert learning to play the American sport of baseball.

ASSESSING STUDENTS' PROCESSING PREDISPOSITIONS

We use different reliable and valid identification instruments to assess students' global versus analytic predispositions (see www.learningstyles.net). However, several personality characteristics apparently differentiate between these two types of processors. These do not always reflect clear lines of demarcation, but they often do.

Textbox 3.1. Comparison of Global vs. Analytic Processing-Style Characteristics

ANALYTIC TENDENCIES	GLOBAL TENDENCIES
Makes decisions based on sequential logic	Makes decisions based on feelings and intuition
Is detail oriented	Sees the *big picture*
Facts and data rule	Imagination rules
Words and tests impress	Symbols and images impress
Emphasizes present and past	Emphasizes present and future
Often excels in math, science, grammar, spelling, and computer technology	Often excels in the arts, philosophy, psychology, and religion
Believes in facts	Believes in emotions; "gets" ideas
Takes pride in knowing	Takes pride in supporting
Appreciates order and patterns	Appreciates spatial perceptions
Understands objects' data and uses	Perceives objects' possibilities
Reality based	Fantasy based
Forms strategies	Presents possibilities
Improves existing things	Creates new things
Practical in orientation	Impetuous, impulsive
Makes safe life choices	Takes risks

GRAPHIC GUIDE TO THE IMPLEMENTATION OF GLOBAL VS. ANALYTIC TEACHING STRATEGIES

Introducing global and analytic teaching strategies should follow immediately after students' learning styles are assessed and a shared understanding of learning-style differences is developed. Accommodating processing-style differences often requires minimal instructional resource development, but calls for some creative planning! (see Textbox 3.2.)

Textbox 3.2. Where Do Global vs. Analytic Teaching Strategies Fit into the Learning-Styles Implementation Process?

STAGE 1

Learning-Styles Assessment
(See www.learningstyles.net for age-appropriate identification tests)

- Share information with students, parents, all teachers.
- Help students use LS profiles and study guides to become self-directed learners.
- Raise awareness about time-of-day energy levels.
- *Make adaptations for global vs. analytic teaching.*

REFLECTION POINTS

1. Consider the global strategies suggested in this chapter and compare them with your most successful, most attention-holding lessons! Why do these lessons work for your students?
2. Think of at least three ways you might persuade a colleague or two to move away from step-by-step instructional approaches and enhance their teaching with global introductions at least occasionally.
3. Create a model lesson that infuses both global and analytic approaches simultaneously. Share your plan with colleagues and ask for feedback.

Answers to What Made the Introduction to This Chapter Global

- The lesson was introduced with a story.
- The story was related to the concept she wanted them to learn.
- The lesson provided a sense of purpose for mastering the material.
- A related assignment could have provided some opportunity for students to discover some information on their own.
- The facts were related to a theme or story and to experiences that should be familiar to the students.

Chapter Four

Redesigning the Classroom for Increased Comfort and Concentration

Everyone knows what typical school classrooms look like. Students' desks and chairs are in rows equally distant from each other, and the teacher's desk is placed where every child can be seen. Because most classrooms resemble each other, imagine Sue Ellen Smith's delight when the principal of her new school brought her to the seventh-grade class to which she'd been assigned. This was like no classroom Sue Ellen had ever seen before!

The size of the room was just like those in Sue Ellen's former school. However *this* one seemed liked a combined club, den, library, living room, and resource center! Students were purposefully moving about while individuals, pairs, and small groups engaged in different activities:

- Four were playing a tic-tac-toe-type Floor Game with their shoes off while reading and answering questions about the U.S. Constitution.
- Under a red and white striped canopy stretched over an outdoor, garden-type breakfast corner, four boys were playing a table-top game—apparently in hot competition comparing two sets of possible answers!
- Under an attractive sign that read, WISHING YOU SUCCESS, three teams of two students each were piecing together puzzle cards while matching questions and answers to see which pair could name the amendments most quickly and correctly.
- One young man sat at his desk with an empty shoe box filled with sand. He was practicing the difficult vocabulary required for his social studies unit on the Bill of Rights by printing the words with his fingers, shuffling the box, and then testing himself to see if he could remember them correctly.
- In the next set of desks, two youths were developing a Students' Bill of Rights that paralleled the original but addressed the many items they

thought should be discussed by their Student Council representatives. However, theirs was illustrated to further emphasize their points.
- Eight boys, subdivided into two teams of four each, were working on a Team Learning.
- The teacher sat with a small group of six reviewing their answers to a Circle of Knowledge on the branches of the United States government.
- Four students sat together with two Programmed Learning Sequences labeled The Constitution. Two were listening to a recording that actually read the printed text, whereas the other pair, although in close proximity to each other, was completing the frames' questions independently while they focused on different aspects of the same material.
- A few were standing, many were seated at desks or on the floor, and some kneeled.
- Some were just reading; others were discussing quietly; a few were putting various puzzle-like items together.
- The whiteboard outlined tasks for everyone, but indicated that individuals could follow their own sequence as long as all tasks were completed by 11:00 A.M.

"This looks comfortable," Sue Ellen thought. "Everyone seems relaxed but, at the same time, busy and interested. How do they all know what to do, and how does the teacher know who did what? This sure is different!"

Sue Ellen liked the atmosphere in this new room, but her second thought was, "Are they learning or just playing?" At that moment, the teacher, Mrs. Rosen, disengaged from the Circle of Knowledge group and came to greet the principal and Sue Ellen. "Welcome," she said. "I'm going to explain how we learn here!"

DIVIDE AND CONQUER

Mrs. Rosen explained her belief that students each mastered new and difficult material in their own way according to their personal learning style. Some needed quiet and others actually created their own sound by talking or singing to themselves while concentrating. Some thought better in discussion with peers or by hearing music (without lyrics) or subdued conversation. However, quiet versus sound was only one learning-style element, and there were others. Therefore she had subdivided the room into separate sections in which individuals could work:

1. in almost complete silence or by softly discussing the content together;
2. in bright versus in subdued lighting;

3. with layered versus lightweight clothing;
4. at desks or on the carpeted floor or pillows;
5. alone, in a pair, in a small group, or with their teacher;
6. passively at specific stations or their desk, or moving from one area to another as they completed mini-assignments; and
7. snacking while concentrating if it helped them complete assignments.

And, because she believed that students learned better or less well with different approaches, they could learn in each of those areas:

- by being involved in small-group instructional strategies, listening to audiocassettes or CDs, reading, seeing DVDs, films, PowerPoint presentations, or videos; using the class computers, kinesthetic Floor Games, tactual materials or working directly with their teacher; or writing responses to posed questions; and/or
- with a Contract Activity Package, a Programmed Learning Sequence, or a Multisensory Instructional Package—as long as they each earned 90 or above on the unit test related to what the class was studying.

RULING THE ROOST

Mrs. Rosen further explained that, although students had choices of how they could learn while in class, when she needed or wanted everyone's attention, she would blink the overhead lights. Whenever she blinked those lights, everyone had to stop the activity in which they were involved at the time and come to immediate attention. Anyone who did not respect that rule would forfeit the privilege of working in their learning style.

Furthermore, *how* each person worked depended on the outcomes of the learning-style identification assessment Sue Ellen would take online that morning. That instrument would describe Sue Ellen's strengths and best ways of learning. If Sue Ellen felt uncomfortable learning as that assessment prescribed, she was permitted to experiment with studying as she wished. However, if Sue Ellen did not earn 90 or above on the unit test on which she was focusing, she then would have to follow the prescribed study methods that the computer program generated to see if those improved her scores.

Establishing Rules and Responsibilities

Mrs. Rosen pointed to a colorfully illustrated chart on the wall. It had few words but many symbols. It had the message on it shown in textbox 4.1.

Textbox 4.1. Learning-Styles Rules and Responsibilities

LS Rules and Responsibilities

1. Your LS may **never distract anyone** with a different style.
2. Your **grades have to be better** than before LS use.
3. Always **sit and speak like a lady or a gentleman.**
4. Always speak like **ladies and gentlemen.**
5. Be **respectful** of and **polite** to everyone.
6. Do **not boast to others** about how we learn.

[That is each teacher's choice.]

Mrs. Rosen also explained that capitalizing on each person's learning style is a *privilege*. Privileges are accompanied by *responsibilities*. She allowed her students' the privilege of working in their individual styles. Living up to the rules was each student's responsibility. Therefore, if rules were broken, privileges could be lost.

She also pointed out that new rules would be added as new privileges were granted. For example, when students were first permitted to sit on the floor if they wished to do so, the rule about "sitting like ladies and gentlemen" was added. When they were first permitted to snack while studying, the rule about not boasting to students in other classes was added. As privileges were added, so were responsibilities.

Establishing Goals and Following Through

Mrs. Rosen told Sue Ellen that she held high expectations for all her students. She expected that each would capitalize on his/her learning style to earn the best grades possible. She expected that students would be respectful of each other regardless of how each learned. She also expected that each would work as soberly as possible to master all the requirements for each lesson or unit.

CREATIVITY RELATED TO ACHIEVEMENT

Mrs. Rosen noted that when children translated the information they were learning into a project that they personally created, they could remember the information much better than when they just tried to commit it to memory. Therefore, for every curriculum objective they are assigned, students are required to develop an instructional resource that someone else could use to learn the information. She said she always would list the choices of the items they could make, but the choices would vary and the product they selected had to be submitted on time and done to the best of their ability.

She also told Sue Ellen that some people were very talented, whereas others were only somewhat talented, and others struggled to be creative. As long as the information included in the submitted project was correct and the product itself was neat and well put together, that would be acceptable. When a student produced an outstanding product, extra credits could be earned toward a grade—just as when students who wrote well received higher grades on written assignments. She urged Sue Ellen to experiment making different kinds of products each time she chose an "Activity Alternative." In that way, Mrs. Rosen said, Sue Ellen would either recognize her naturally strongest talents or would develop talent in new areas.

EXPLAINING THE PROGRAM TO PARENTS

Mrs. Rosen asked Sue Ellen to take a note home to her parents, inviting them to visit and learn what learning-styles-based teaching was all about. The note described a little about what happened daily in class, but said that the teacher would be pleased to meet with them and test them both to identify *their* learning styles with an assessment called Building Excellence so that they could compare their styles with Sue Ellen's. "When are you going to identify my learning style?" asked Sue Ellen. "Right now," Mrs. Rosen responded, and she gently guided her newest student toward one of the classroom computers. "You're in for a treat young lady! After this, you'll know just how to study based on your learning-style strengths!"

GRAPHIC GUIDE TO ROOM REDESIGN

Changing the learning environment is an early step in learning-styles implementation. It closely follows assessing students' learning styles and addressing their differences in processing style. Creativity is a plus, practicality is a must! (See Textbox 4.2.) See the samples of redesigned rooms from a variety of international classrooms at the end of this chapter.

Textbox 4.2. Where Does Room Redesign Fit into the Learning-Styles Implementation Process?

STAGE 1

Learning-Styles Assessment
(See www.learningstyles.net for LS assessment tools)

- Share information with students, parents, all teachers.
- Help students use LS profiles and study guides to become self-directed learners.
- Raise awareness about time-of-day energy levels.
- Make adaptations for global vs. analytic teaching.

STAGE 2

Initial Implementation Steps

- *Environmental accommodations (Room redesign)*

REFLECTION POINTS

1. Irvine and York (1995) stated that "All students are capable of learning, provided the learning environment attends to a variety of learning styles" (p. 494). How did this chapter validate their point and your own experiences with more or less traditional classroom environments?
2. Consider at least three environmental accommodations from Mrs. Rosen's classroom presented in this chapter that you might implement in your own classroom.

This is the LEAPS Children's Book Club, one of many classrooms designed to accommodate students' needs for mobility, seating comfort, and varied social groupings. Courtesy of Dr. Pengiran Rahmah Pengiran Jadid and Roz Alia Zin, both associated with LEAPS Educational Services, Learning Style Center in Brunei.

This is but one of the many redesigned classrooms at the Hvalstad School of the Asker Municipality, Norway. Courtesy of Dr. Tone Guldahl.

This is a view of the Library Periodicals Corner in St. George's School, Wanganui, New Zealand. Courtesy of Charlotte Humphrey.

Classroom detail from BÝLFEN Private Schools, Istanbul, Turkey. Courtesy of Sebahat Basusta and Kaan Sagnak.

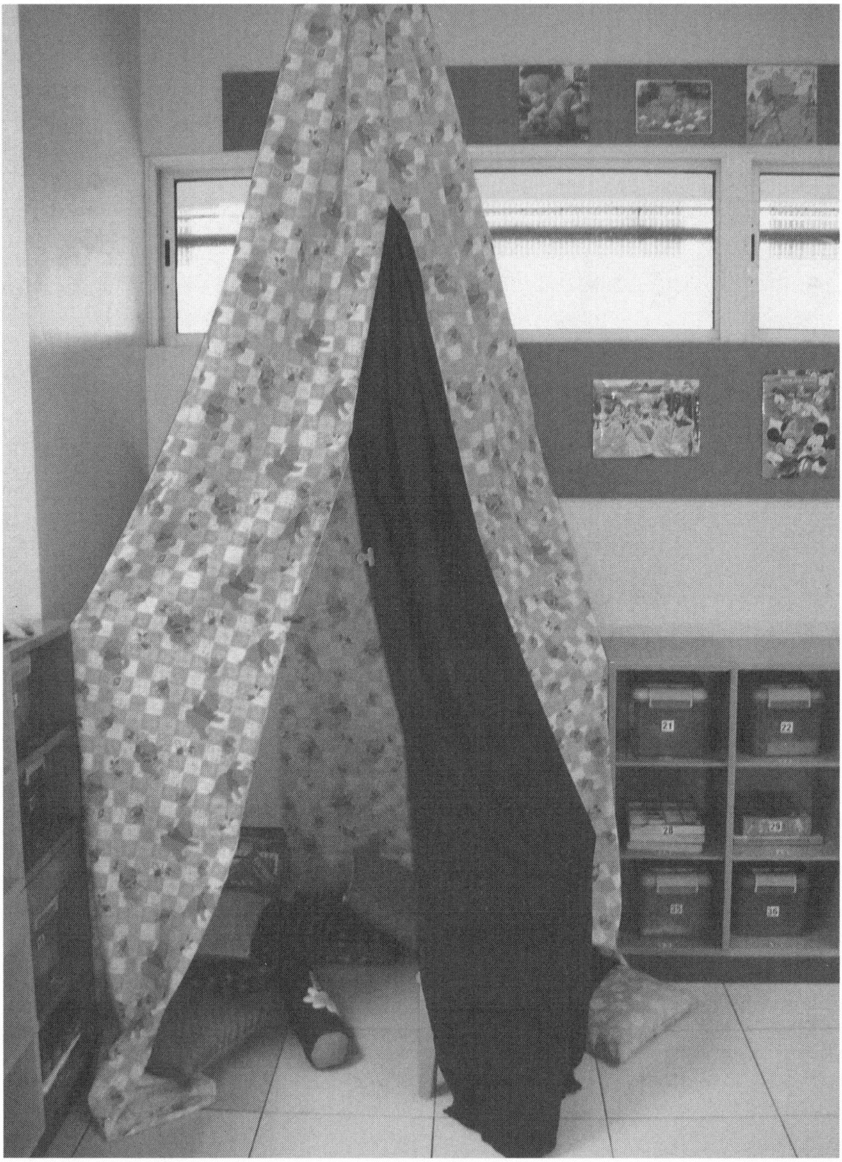

This is a kindergarten Reading Corner in St. Paul College, Pasiq, Manila, The Philippines. Courtesy of Sister Teresita Baricaua, SPC, Directress.

This depicts one of the second-grade "Flip This Classroom Project" redesigns in the Van Cortlandville Elementary School, Lakeland Central School District, Shrub Oak, New York. Courtesy of Dr. Lois Favre and Susan Rundle.

Chapter Five

Teaching Tactual Students Tactually

Kyle, a bright-eyed, motivated, but struggling fourth grader knows very well what is expected of him: In each of his previous years of schooling, teachers often reminded him of the same, "Eyes on me! Keep your hands to yourself!" If only he could help himself. His hands seem to constantly fidget, mostly because they need to touch something while he is trying to pay attention. Kyle truly doesn't intend to be mean when he pulls on Jessica's hair; but she sits right in front of him and, somehow, his fingers end up entangled in her pretty curls. Indeed, Kyle's fingers often become involved with someone or something he is not supposed be touching.

After repeated discussions with Kyle and conferences with him and his parents, this touching problem was brought to the assistant principal, Mrs. Robinson. She suggested that "prevention is worth a pound of cure" and Kyle's teachers were urged to "identify strategies to *prevent* him from getting into trouble." One solution Mrs. Robinson suggested was to engage Kyle in hands-on instruction designed to help him master the curriculum. Another was the use of a commercially available squeeze ball to keep his hands busy.

What proved to be the most effective approach his teacher eventually tried was to show Kyle (and a few others in the class who frequently snapped or tapped their fingers or who couldn't keep their hands to themselves) how to create his own instructional resources. These not only kept the frenetic youngsters out of trouble, but also helped them master challenging grade-level content.

Kyle thrived on the manipulatives he created, and he completed fourth grade with more academic success than his parents thought possible. Although his fingers occasionally wandered from purposeful tasks, Kyle learned to concentrate without intruding on classmates and, at the same time, reduced his need for fidgeting.

CHARACTERISTICS OF STUDENTS WITH TACTUAL PREFERENCES

There are children like Kyle in almost every class, be it a mainstream, inclusion, resource center, or self-contained Special Education room. They are there because many boys (and some girls) tend to be highly tactual and/or in need of frequent (if not constant) mobility. Their ability to remember at least 70% of what they hear or read is unlikely to be as biologically well developed or favored. Such youth often struggle and fall behind in traditional classes where teachers mostly rely on direct instruction using audio-visual delivery to teach. Even if advanced technology is used—such as PowerPoint presentations or video streaming—tactual learners need more than the highly stimulating visual support these resources offer.

HOW DO TACTUAL LEARNERS LEARN?

Engaging tactual learners' *minds* by getting their *hands* onto manipulative instructional resources is one certain way to involve them actively in new and difficult information successfully. Why do tactual resources "work" when other strategies have not? Precisely because these children's strongest perceptual modality is tactual. When a runner runs, he does well. When a singer sings, he also does well. But when a runner sings or a singer runs, it is difficult for either to measure up to colleagues with the opposite skills or talents. Learners with only tactual strengths usually are neither auditory/word nor visual/word learners (as we teachers assume everyone ought to be!). However, they often are visual/picture attentive. Therefore, all tactual resources should include colorful pictures that reflect the content to be learned.

Tactual resources alone may not necessarily produce the increased achievement we want for at-risk youngsters. Reinforcing required information or skills through these students' secondary and tertiary perceptual preferences ensure that they master the required material. Don't try to reinforce for them through an auditory or visual/text approach. Getting them involved and interested in learning tactually is the first step. To have them remember what they are learning, reinforce the content with a kinesthetic Floor Game (see chapter 6). If you are willing to try this dual suggestion only once, you will see the difference in such students' retention, attitudes toward learning, and behaviors.

GETTING STARTED WITH TACTUAL RESOURCES

Many at-risk students cannot sit for verbal presentations; their listening attention spans are limited to just a few minutes. Such youth concentrate and internalize only when actively engaged with hands-on approaches. Create one or more of the following resources and see how interested (and well behaved) your students become!

In the beginning, make a few of these manipulatives yourself—or collaborate with colleagues to create several on a topic you all teach. Use these resources individually with highly tactual students or place them into learning centers. The next week, teach students to make their own tactual materials with the same directions and templates explained below. Students will learn through the process of seeking information and transferring it onto their tactual resources; they also will value and take good care of their resources. Students may share or swap their resources with classmates to reinforce the content. They may use them at their desks or wherever you specify in the classroom or at home. Thus, students' environmental preferences can be addressed at the same time they are learning through their perceptual strengths. Tactual resources also can be used to respond to students' sociological preferences for learning independently, in pairs, or in a small group.

DESCRIPTION OF TACTUAL RESOURCES AND HOW TO CREATE THEM

Pic-A-Holes

Pic-A-Holes can be created in a number of different ways (see Dunn & Dunn, 1992, 1993, 1999; Dunn, Dunn, & Perrin, 1994). They are ideal for learning and/or reinforcing new information and as multiple-choice test preparation tools. As such, they represent a refreshing departure from dittos and practice-test booklets that most schools provide. We recommend the use of an inexpensive two-pocket folder for the Pic-A-Hole holder and five-by-eight-inch index cards for the Question Cards. Follow Template (A) of figure 5.1 below to create the folder by cutting a large opening for the questions and punching three or four holes (as you choose) for possible answers all the way through.

Use the five-by-eight-inch index cards to create Question Cards following Template (B). Be certain you cut *through* the hole for the correct answer on each index card. Place all Question Cards into the case and provide a golf-tee or chopstick for students to insert into their choice of the correct answer. When the golf tee is placed into the correct answer, the card should be removable. It will not come out if an incorrect answer is selected (see figure 5.1).

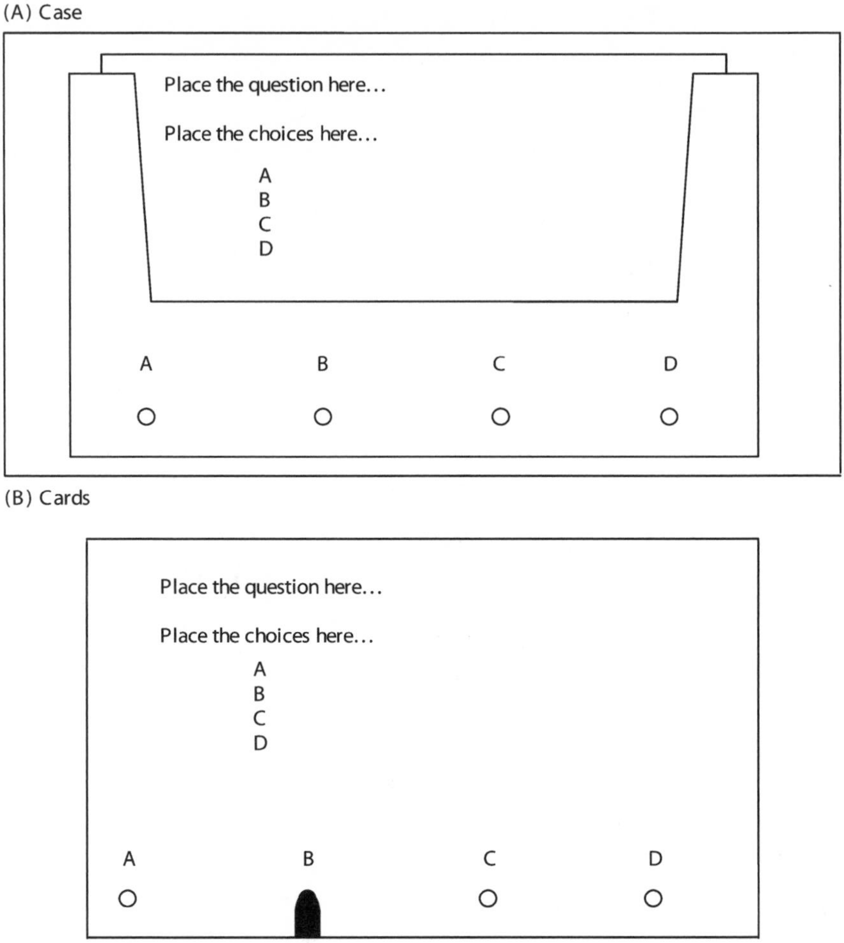

Figure 5.1. Pic-A-Hole Templates A and B

Learning Circles

Most worksheets contain matching activities, questions, or problems with short answers that can be turned into a Learning Circle. Cut two large circles out of poster board or oak tag. Divide the circle into 6 to 10 sections (depending on the complexity of the task, your students' ages, or their readiness levels). Add a question or problem to each section of the circle. Use a corresponding number of clothespins (or Velcro) to identify the correct answer for each of the questions or problems. Your students' task is to match the Learning-Circle sections to the best answers on the clothespins. One way to

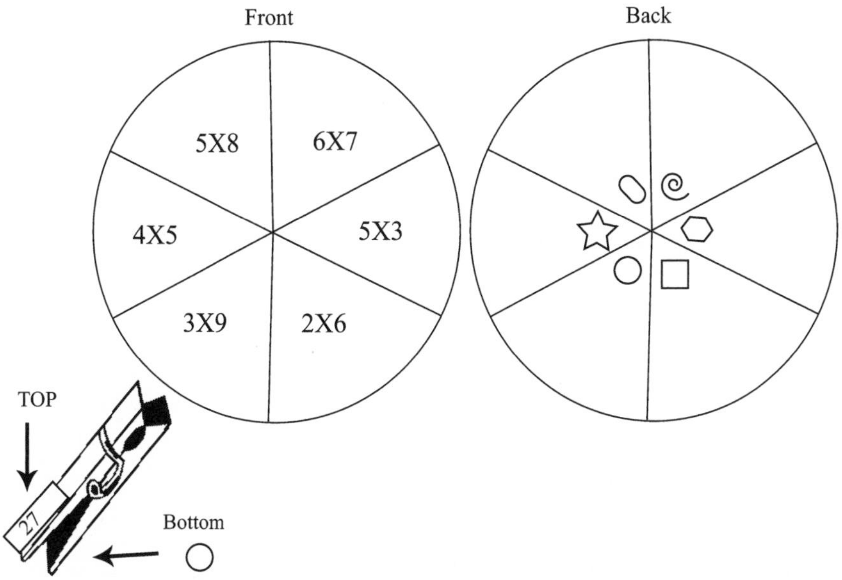

Figure 5.2. Learning Circle Template

make the resource self-corrective is by color- or picture-coding the back of the Learning Circle and the back of the clothespins (see figure 5.2).

Task Cards

Task Cards also are easy to make and self-corrective. These resources can be used to introduce new material to tactual learners or to review previously taught content to kinesthetic learners. Task Cards are designed as simple puzzles and present information about a specific topic, concept, or skill by translating it into questions and answers, words and definitions, and so on. Multipart Task Cards may carry three or more different types of information, such as (a) a word, (b) a definition, and (c) an illustration. Each card is cut into irregularly shaped sections so that only the matching pieces fit together (see figure 5.3).

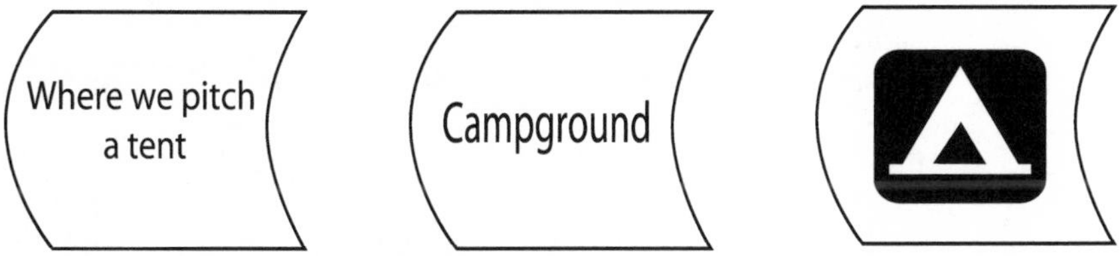

Figure 5.3. Sample Vocabulary Task Card

Flip Chutes

Flip Chutes are possibly the most captivating of all the tactual resources presented here. They are made with used (but washed) half-gallon milk or juice containers combined with an inside chute and small cards. The container is magically transformed into an apparatus that flips the inserted card over and thus provides the correct answer to anyone using this devise (see figure 5.4).

To construct your first Flip Chute, use a half-gallon juice or milk container and follow the directions below (adapted from Dunn, Dunn, & Perrin, 1994):

1. Remove the top of a milk or juice container.
2. Cut the side folds of the top portion down to the top of the container.
3. On the front edge, measure down both 1½ inches and 2½ inches. Draw lines across the container. Remove that area.
4. Mark up from the bottom 1½ inches and 2½ inches. Draw lines across the container. Remove that space.
5. Cut one 5 x 8 inch index card to measure 6½ inches by 3½ inches.
6. Cut a second index card to measure 7½ inches by 3½ inches.
7. Fold down ½ inch at both ends of the smaller strip. Fold down ½ inch at one end of the longer strip.
8. Insert the smaller strip into the bottom opening with the folded edge resting on the upper portion of the bottom opening. Attach it securely with masking tape.
9. Bring the upper part of the smaller strip out through the upper opening, with the folded part going down over the center section of the carton. Attach it with masking tape.
10. Work with the longer strip; one end is folded down and the other end is unfolded. Insert the unfolded end of the longer strip into the bottom opening of the container from the outside. Be certain that the strip goes up along the back of the container. Push it into the container until the folded part rests on the bottom part of the container. Attach it with masking tape.
11. Attach the upper edge of the longer strip to the back of the container creating a slide. Secure it with masking tape about ⅝ of an inch from the top of the carton.
12. Fold down the top flaps of the container and tape them in place, forming a rectangular box.
13. Use small, 2 x 2½ inch index cards to write the question on one side and the answer upside down on the flip side. Notch each question side at the top right to insure appropriate positioning when the student uses the card.

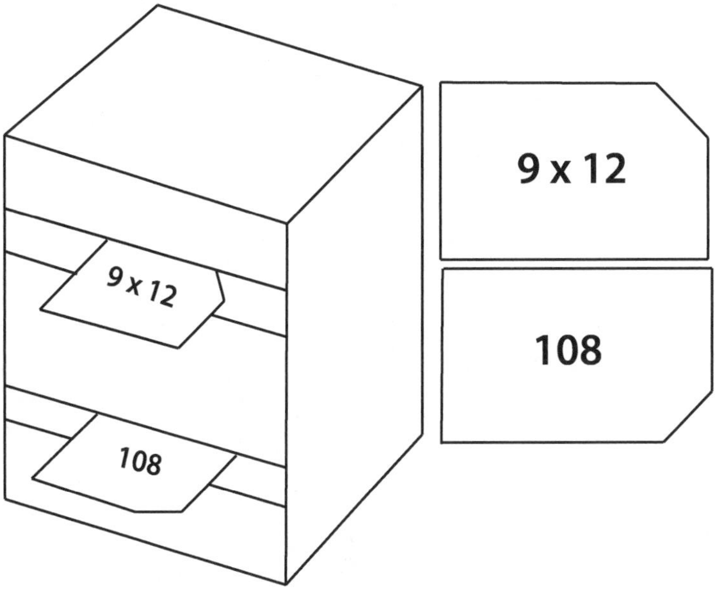

Figure 5.4. How the Flip Chute Works

Electroboards

Electroboards are teacher- and student-created electronic gadgets that offer a learning experience that truly mesmerizes most youngsters. The instructional tool itself could be produced professionally or simply by using everyday household items. We recommend that you start with a manila folder. Enter questions on the left side of the folder and answers on its right side. Punch holes and insert a brass fastener in front of each question and answer. Open the folder and connect the matching questions and answers with thin strips of tinfoil. Cover each foil strip with masking tape before moving to the next one. Once all the electric circuits are established and carefully covered with masking tape, close and seal the folder to hide the taped foil. All you need is an inexpensive continuity tester, which lights up when its two prongs are touched to matching questions and answers (see figure 5.5).

SAMPLE TACTUAL RESOURCES DESIGNED FOR AT-RISK STUDENTS

Below are sample photographs from Maria Dove's classroom. She taught a unit on the water cycle to her students and found that a variety of tactual

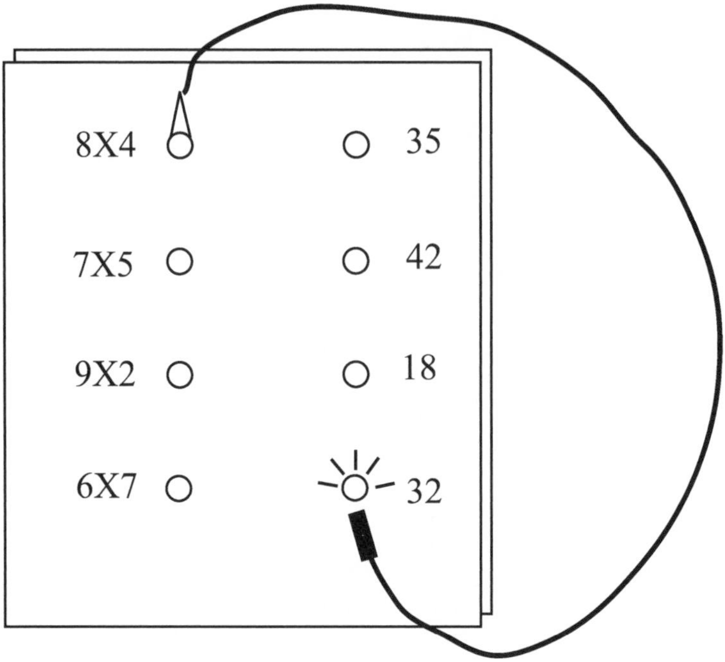

Figure 5.5. Electroboard Template

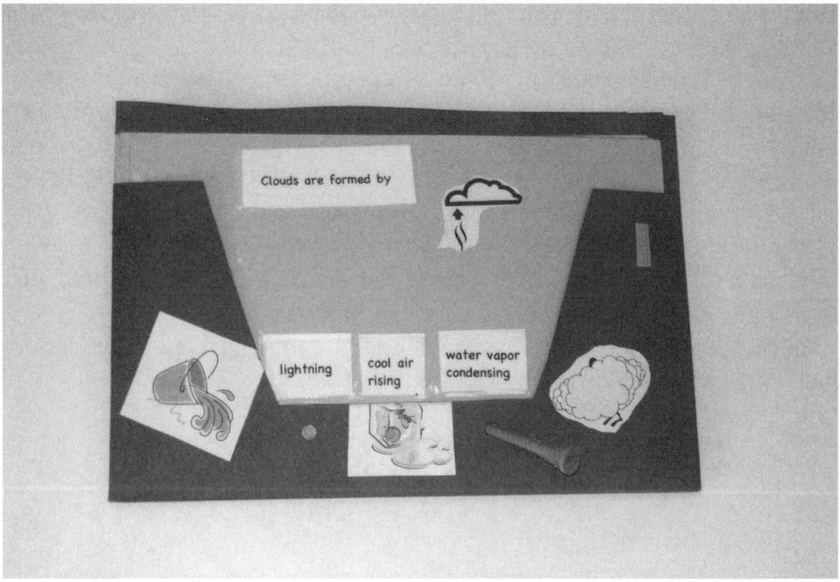

Water Cycle Pic-A-Hole.

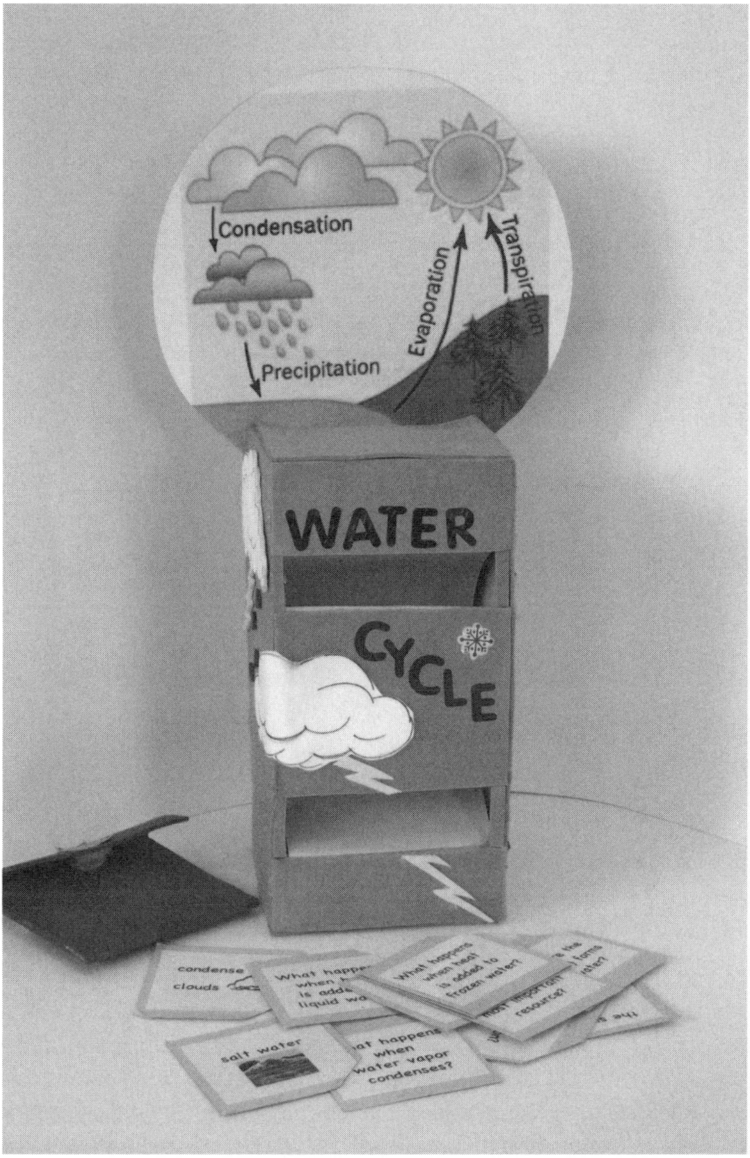

Water Cycle Flip Chute.

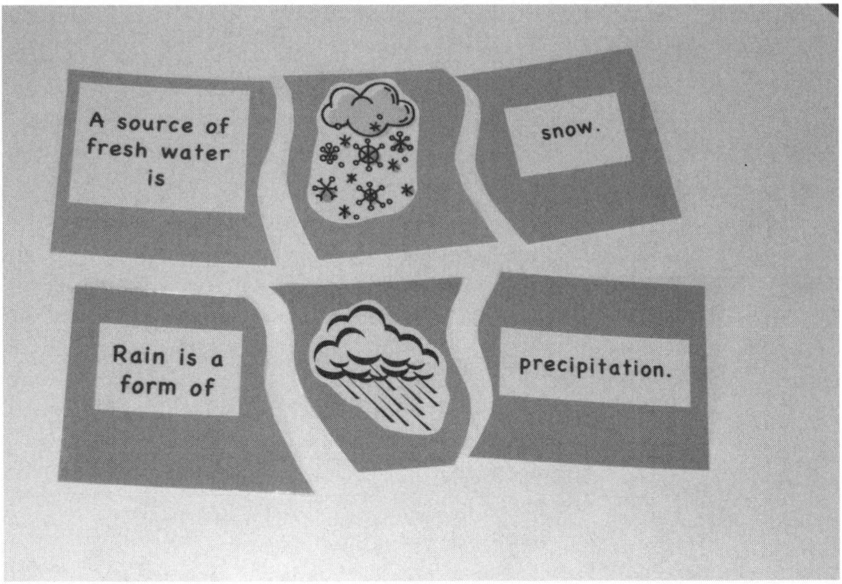

Water Cycle Task Cards.

resources, both teaching and then reteaching various aspects of the water cycle, helped her students master the content effectively.

ASSESSING STUDENT PERFORMANCE

Using Tactual Resources for Self-Assessment

The tactual resources described in this chapter can be used in a variety of settings and adjusted to accommodate additional learning-style preferences (environmental, sociological, and physiological). They are game-like, motivating, self-corrective tools. As such, these resources lend themselves to student self-assessment. Since each resource is designed to have a built-in self-corrective feature, there is no need for teachers to provide immediate feedback on student performance; the resources themselves allow learners to gauge their own level of conceptual understanding and, thus, permit them to self-assess and self-correct automatically. Too, because they may be used in pairs or in small groups of three, these resources allow students who cannot master the objectives independently to do so with peers.

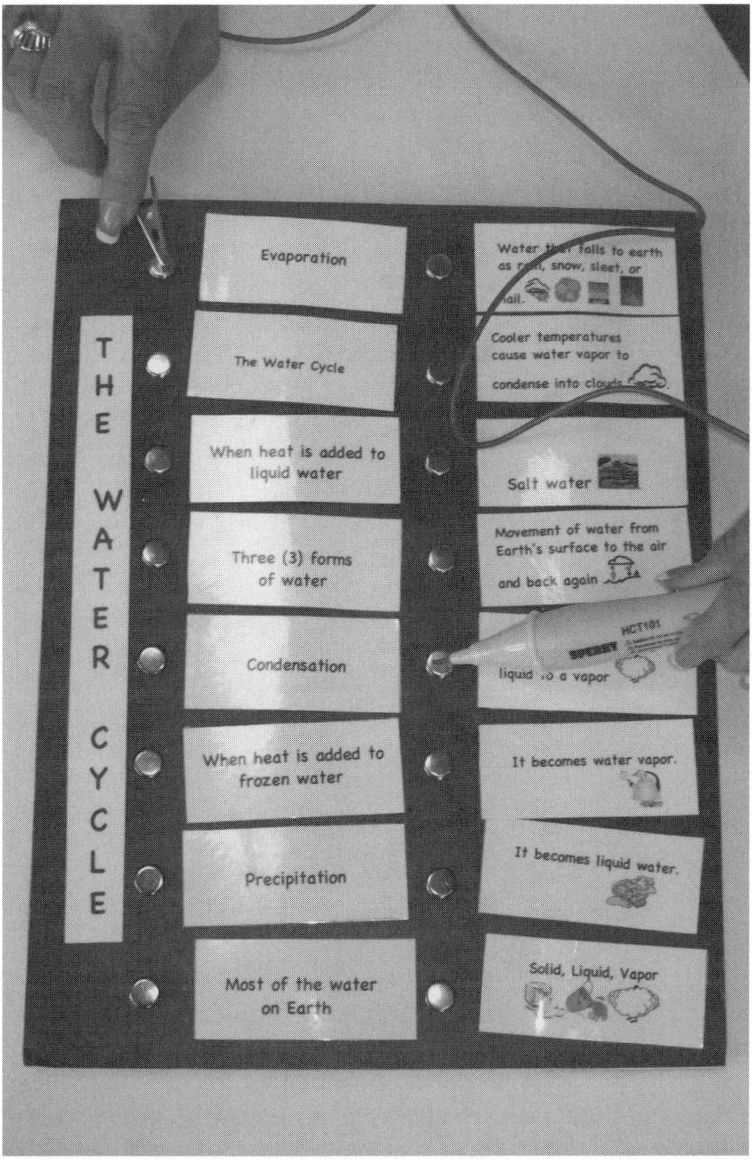

Water Cycle Electroboard.

Textbox 5.1. Sample Rubric to Assess Student-Created Tactual Resources

Dimensions	Excellent job!	You are on track!	You need to work on this!
Content	There are no mistakes in the content.	There are minor mistakes in the content.	There are several mistakes in the content.
Design	You followed directions very closely! This tactual resource looks perfect!	You followed directions most of the time. Your resource looks fine!	You followed directions only some of the time. Your resource needs to be refined!
Spelling and Punctuation	Perfect spelling!	Hardly any mistakes!	Check your spelling and punctuation; too many mistakes!
Ease of Usage	Everything works well!	Most things work most of the time!	Some resources are inoperable.

Assessing Student-Created Tactual Resources

We strongly recommend that students be encouraged to create their own tactual resources. If they do so, assess the content and format of each resource by using a simple rubric (see textbox 5.1). This baseline rubric can be modified to provide additional guidelines for creating each specific tactual resource or can be used holistically as indicated herein.

Teaching Creatively; Assessing Traditionally

In this age of high-stakes and regularly administered standardized tests, teachers often wonder how to best prepare their students while simultaneously continuing with their best classroom practices. Sheehan (2008) encouraged his graduate education majors to "teach creatively, yet assess traditionally." Similarly, we firmly believe that all of the above tactual resources may serve as alternatives to standardized test preparation materials and yield better results for the highly tactual students who are likely to be unable to stay focused on lengthy, printed matter. As they master the content, skill, or concept nontraditionally by using tactual resources, you will see that their skills become transferred to more traditional testing formats as the much-dreaded standardized assessment date approaches!

Textbox 5.2. Where Do Tactual Resources Fit into the Learning-Styles Implementation Process?

STAGE 1

Learning-Styles Assessment
(See www.learningstyles.net for LS assessment tools)

- Share information with students, parents, all teachers.
- Help students use LS profiles and study guides to become self-directed learners.
- Raise awareness about time-of-day energy levels.
- Make adaptations for global vs. analytic teaching.

STAGE 2

Initial Implementation Steps

- Environmental accommodations (Room redesign)
- *Methodologies and resources to respond to perceptual preferences: Tactual resources*

GRAPHIC GUIDE TO THE IMPLEMENTATION OF TACTUAL RESOURCES

Tactual resources should be introduced into the instructional process in the early stages, right after or along with environmental modifications. Tactual resources can also help students with or without other learning-style responsive strategies because they will encourage students' active engagement in the learning process (see textbox 5.2).

REFLECTION POINTS

1. Review the Dunn and Dunn model and explore which learning-style preferences, in addition to the perceptual, can be addressed while using tactual resources in your classroom.
2. Consider the connection between using tactual resources and differentiating instruction in the classroom. In which way(s) can manipulatives help scaffold instruction and meet individual learning needs?
3. Explain why it is important to add illustrations or pictures to the tactual resources.

Chapter Six

Teaching Kinesthetic Students Kinesthetically

> If a man does not keep pace with his companions, perhaps it is because he hears a different drummer. Let him step to the music . . . he hears, however measured or far away.—Henry David Thoreau

Thoreau must have been thinking of Sam, a bright, energetic, helpful young man in Mrs. Doyle's fifth-grade class. Surely Sam hears a different drummer because he walks, waffles, waltzes, or wiggles in class during the entire school day. When it comes to rotating students' chores, Sam is happy to be the class monitor or materials manager—or whatever permits him to move without generating criticism. He willingly delivers all notes and messages to the farthest corners of the school building, straightens bookcases or supplies, and/or distributes resources for the entire class efficiently and effortlessly.

However, when everyone is required to sit quietly, Sam stands, saunters, or slithers in his own private area near his desk. When he agrees to stay seated, Sam rocks his chair, barely escaping dangerous falls. He always is among the first to volunteer to dramatize a scene from language arts or social studies readings. He "comes alive" when he recounts stories or goes to the board to write answers (even if they aren't always correct!) He loves charades, science experiments, and class trips—his most eagerly anticipated activities. Surprisingly, Sam remembers every detail of what he is supposed to learn while engaged in tasks. And no one is more excited or positive about the school's annual field day!

After months of struggling to keep him in his seat, Mrs. Doyle felt she was in a real bind. Fifth grade is packed with standardized tests, so how would Sam ever master the required curriculum given his constant need to move or to stand? This year, however, Sam was assigned a seat near the door, somewhat apart from his classmates. His desk is slightly taller than the others so he can stand and lean on it as he completes schoolwork. Now, for the first time during standardized testing, no one has to remind him to stay seated or reprimand him for forgetting to do so; Sam is permitted to stand. The results are remarkable.

CHARACTERISTICS OF STUDENTS WITH KINESTHETIC PREFERENCES

Sam is known by teachers and administrators as "the energized kid who cannot sit still!" But should he be expected to? Sam and those who process information better while on their feet, always seem to be in motion and cannot sit while paying attention to teachers for extended periods of time. These youngsters cannot read, write, or listen to teacher-directed lessons while required to remain in one place with their hands folded and their feet on the floor!

The Sams of our world truly are at risk of falling behind academically; they often are mislabeled "hyperactive." They really do learn best on their feet and are able to make lasting connections among concepts, their applications, and comprehensive learning while moving as opposed to while stationary. Their auditory and visual perceptual skills may not be as developed or favored as their kinesthetic modality. Often they also seem to have stronger than average tactual strengths as well (see chapter 5).

DESCRIPTION OF KINESTHETIC RESOURCES AND LEARNING ACTIVITIES

Kinesthetic activities are required for people who profit from instructional experiences that engage their bodies as well as their minds. These resources are designed to be self-corrective and used independently, in pairs, or in small groups of three or four. If teacher supervised, they can be used with the entire class. If designed as Floor Games or Wall Games, they can be placed into Learning Stations or stored and unrolled as needed for placement in any empty space in the room or hall. These instructional resources are fun and can be adapted to any content, grade, or ability level.

Students with kinesthetic preferences or strengths learn best when permitted to stand, move about, or actively interact with other students. They function well even when writing on the chalk- or whiteboard or drawing on large sheets of chart paper when Brainstorming (see chapter 7). Allowing kinesthetically inclined students (usually males) to think while participating in Floor, Wall, or Table-Top Games, demonstrations, dramatizations, role-playing, or skits activates their large motor skills and enhances their retention of complex content.

Design lessons that include Gallery Walks, which invite students to visit various exhibits placed around the room on whatever wall space you have available. Encourage students to generate questions or problems in small groups and then have a representative member of each team "walk" the question or problem over to the adjacent team. Once exposed to Floor or Wall Games, students should be permitted to design their own instructional activities, just as we advised when describing tactual resources. Use the following strategies and experiment with kinesthetic teaching in your room. You will find that restless, overactive students, and many lethargic youth will become engaged in participatory learning—particularly when they are not only *permitted*, but actually *required*, to move!

HOW TO GET STARTED WITH KINESTHETIC RESOURCES

Because kinesthetic students often do not function well with traditional teaching, try the following nontraditional, creative activities to enhance their large motor skills and encourage whole-body involvement.

1. Create giant wall or floor diagrams with masking tape and have students literally *walk* through the key concepts.
2. On either the wall or floor, create large maps for students to explore, color rivers and mountain ranges, and name interesting sites to visit. It is easy to enlarge and then project book maps onto large sheets of paper from the original source if you use an overhead projector some distance from the wall on which you have hung either paper or a large, old plastic curtain, sheet, or tablecloth you no longer need.
3. Project diagrams, maps, or graphic outlines onto the wall for students to illustrate, label, or use as a basis for historical stories they create and dramatize.
4. Prepare easy-to-follow prompts for real-life role-plays related to the target content.
5. Collect and make available everyday household objects and unusual props such as hats for skits or dramatizations or place mats on the floor at equal distances from each other to form a hopscotch game for reinforcing grammar, math, science, social studies, or vocabulary facts.
6. Make available chalkboards, dry-erase boards, or flip charts for student use when they are creating games.

7. Set aside time for charades and pantomimes to permit students to express themselves physically but politely.
8. Label different parts of the classroom for instructional purposes and direct students to respond to questions by moving from one designated area to another.
9. Enable students to practice for tests by labeling the four corners of the room A, B, C, and D and having classmates respond to practice questions by directing them to move "ahead" from one corner to the next based on the difficulty or complexity of questions worth different amounts of points.
10. Place images or quotations around the classroom and have student teams walk from one to another to choose the image or statement they can respond to.
11. Have students line up alphabetically by their first or last names or by their birthdates from January to December. Once a straight line has been formed, "fold" the line in half by first pairing the students at each end of the line, then the next two, and so forth. When students each have a partner, allow them to discuss a pre-established question in pairs while they remain standing with that person. They then need to draw or illustrate their best-paired answers so that other pairs can decipher their drawings.

HOW TO DESIGN FLOOR, WALL, OR TABLE-TOP GAMES

Effective ways for incorporating kinesthetic learning into any classroom is by designing body-action Floor Games. If floor space is limited, the same games can be used as Wall Games or Table-Top Games. Follow these simple suggestions and you will take a giant step toward fun-filled learning for your most active students. You'll also involve the timid and shy ones.

1. Decide on the content (information or skill) that you will incorporate into the game.
2. Select a well-known game design (snake path, tic-tac-toe, twister) or devise your own original template.
3. Generate many questions related to the target content either alone or with your students.
4. Transfer the questions onto index cards. Print and have students illustrate the correct answers on the back of each card.

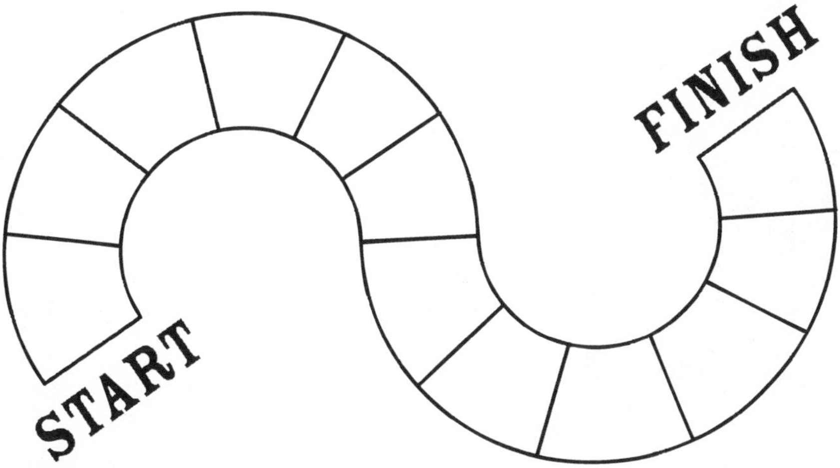

Figure 6.1. Snake Path Template

This Floor Game, tucked away into a quiet nook, permits kinesthetic learners to either introduce or reinforce required information independently or with a classmate or two—or more! This is one of the hundreds of Floor Games in daily use at the Hvalstad School of the Asker Municipality, Norway. Courtesy of Dr. Tone Guldahl.

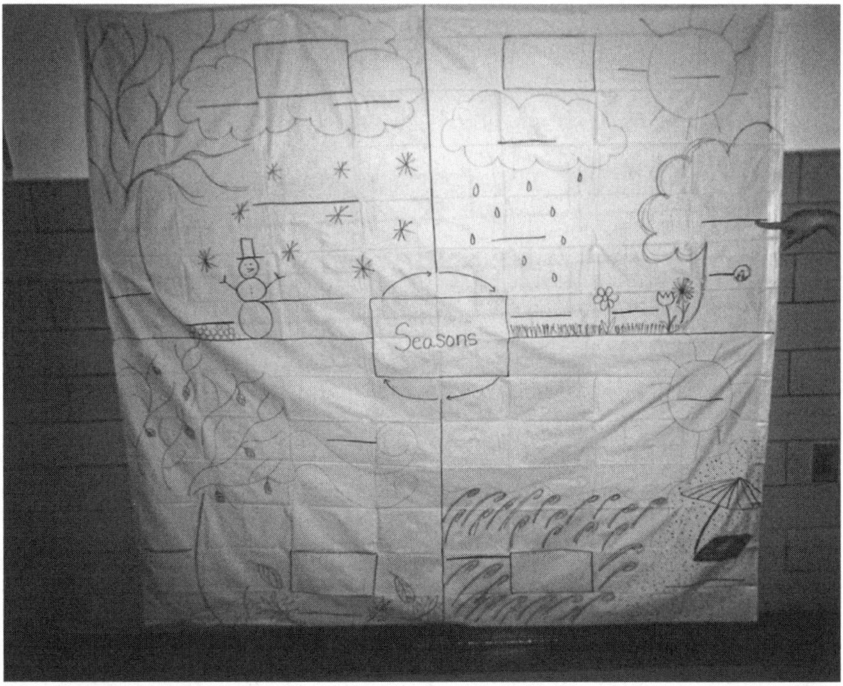

This is a Four Seasons Labeling Wall Game *produced by Jennifer Ecuyer at the North Bellmore Teacher Center, New York. For students (and teachers) who do not enjoy bending, hopping, or skipping on a Floor Game, a similar physical effect can be obtained by mounting the game on one of the classroom walls and learning while standing. Courtesy of Eileen Ward.*

5. Collaboratively establish the rules for the game. Once a question is answered correctly, the student is empowered to make a move forward on the Floor Game. Have students play the game in pairs or teams against each other (see figure 6.1).

SAMPLE KINESTHETIC ACTIVITIES DESIGNED FOR AT-RISK STUDENTS

- In a kindergarten classroom, the teacher regularly takes her students on *imaginary walks*. They are asked to stand and walk in place near their desks as she invites them to close their eyes and enter her *magic forest*, a new *space station*, or an *underwater kingdom*—her fairy tale for the day! Students move their bodies to avoid crashing into meteors, duck to miss gigantic flying bugs, or hop or swim in place to reach the surface of the ocean.

- After each student generates a set of index cards with their required vocabulary words on one side and original illustrated definitions on the back, one elementary school teacher divides her fourth graders into two equal groups. Since the students are familiar with this routine, half the class forms a circle immediately. They know that once the circle is created, they need to turn facing outward. The students in the remaining group each come up to the circle to be assigned a partner. The students then are ready to play.

  The index cards are pulled out; the inside circle tests the outside circle on the vocabulary words, and then the roles are reversed. After a few minutes of practice, the outside circle is signaled to move down one person while the inside circle stays in place. As new pairs are formed, the process is repeated. Students test each other by providing correct definitions for their vocabulary words. This inside-outside circle formation is also ideal for checking on reading comprehension, preparing for spelling quizzes, or reviewing math problems using mental math in which partners test each other on the assigned material.
- In a seventh-grade social studies class, students spend a lot of time examining historical papers to be able to answer document-based questions (DBQs) on their annual standardized assessments. Instead of completing one ditto after another, their teacher recreates the DBQ exam as a Gallery Walk. He places eight enlarged documents (cartoons, quotes, pictures, historical photographs, and short paragraphs) around the classroom and distributes a DBQ response sheet that requires students to answer any five essential questions from among an itemized list. Students are encouraged to work independently, in pairs, or in small groups as they wish.
- In preparation for an eighth-grade ELA test, an English teacher designed a Wall Game using a tic-tac-toe template. Two teams compete to name

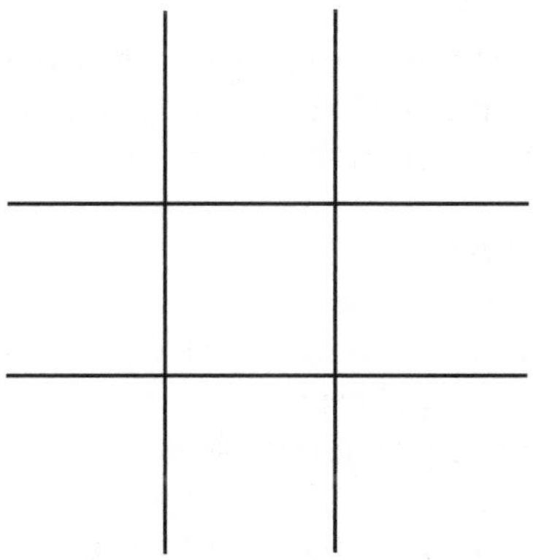

Figure 6.2. Tic-Tac-Toe Template

the literary element in the excerpts assigned. Once the literary element is correctly identified, the team is allowed to place an X or O on an erasable tic-tac-toe board mounted on the wall (see figure 6.2).

HOW TO ADDRESS AUDITORY, VISUAL, TACTUAL, VERBAL, AND KINESTHETIC PERCEPTUAL STRENGTHS AT THE SAME TIME: CHOICES, CHOICES, CHOICES!

One way to allow all students to use their perceptual strengths is by giving them choices when responding to a task. For example, after reading Jack Prelutsky's (1983) poem, "Me I Am," students may choose how they wish to express their reactions. They are invited to share what is personally unique about themselves in any way they see fit. They may draw pictures (tactual/global), write a story or poem (tactual/analytic), create a song (tactual/musical), pantomime (kinesthetic), create a clay figure (tactual), or dance (kinesthetic) to express their uniqueness.

Elementary teachers often incorporate Learning Centers or Stations into their class environments. Regardless of the name used for this strategy, kinesthetic students of all ages who need mobility benefit from a learning-style-based arrangement in which they can approach the same content in different classroom areas. Initially, students are grouped according to their primary perceptual strengths and begin their involvement wherever each is most likely to successfully master the content. They gradually are redirected to two additional class sections to reinforce the identical content in alternative ways.

In the Media Center, auditory students *listen* to recorded material as they follow printed textbooks or worksheets. With permission, some listen to podcasts via the Internet. In the Library Center, other students explore text- and image-based resources such as books, diagrams, encyclopedias, illustrations, PowerPoint presentations, or any other visual source. In the Exploration Center, teacher- and student-created manipulatives such as multipart Task Cards, Flip Chutes, and Electroboards—all are available for either initial learning or reinforcement (Dunn & Dunn, 1992, 1993, 1999; Dunn, Dunn, & Perrin, 1994).

In the Discussion Center, students with a strong need for verbalizing are involved in a guided discussion on the topic. Finally, in the Learn-On-Your-Feet Center, students play a Table-Top or Floor Game as they answer questions related to the content.

In addition, Contract Activity Packages are available to accommodate students' various learning styles and perceptual preferences by offering them choices. Activity and Reporting Alternatives are created to align with all major perceptual preferences (see chapter 8).

ASSESSING STUDENT PERFORMANCE

Kinesthetic activities—similar to those that are tactual—are most effective for self- and informal assessments. Tactual resources, Floor Games, and Table-Top Games always are designed to be self-corrective. As such, they can be used both for introducing, reviewing, or self-assessing content knowledge and skills.

By assigning values such as *agree*, *disagree*, *strongly agree*, or *strongly disagree* to each of the four corners of the room with a sign indicating that decision, informal assessment becomes kinesthetic and fun. The teacher poses a statement or question to which students are required to consider and determine their decision. Students then move to the corner of the room with the designation with which they most identify. They then can verbally challenge each other by explaining their reasoning.

Textbox 6.1. Where Do Kinesthetic Resources Fit into the Learning-Styles Implementation Process?

STAGE 1

Learning-Styles Assessment
(See www.learningstyles.net for LS assessment tools)

- Share information with students, parents, all teachers.
- Help students use LS profiles and study guides to become self-directed learners.
- Raise awareness about time-of-day energy levels.
- Make adaptations for global vs. analytic teaching.

STAGE 2

Initial Implementation Steps

- Environmental accommodations (Room redesign)
- *Methodologies and resources to respond to perceptual preferences: Kinesthetic Floor Games*

GRAPHIC GUIDE TO THE IMPLEMENTATION OF KINESTHETIC RESOURCES

Kinesthetic resources should be introduced into the instructional process in the very beginning, immediately after tactual resources. Indeed, you could use kinesthetic resources with students, with or without other learning-style responsive strategies because they will help students learn and simultaneously enjoy being in your class (see textbox 6.1).

REFLECTION POINTS

1. Albert Einstein is attributed the saying, "Learning is experience. Everything else is just information." Consider the relevance of this observation to this chapter and your own teaching.
2. Name at least four reasons why kinesthetic learning should be used with at-risk students and four strategies for implementing these activities in your classroom.

Chapter Seven

Teaching Peer-Motivated Students with Small-Group Techniques

Dr. Martin broached the topic of "differentiating instruction" to his staff. He suggested that a variety of small-group techniques would "engage students more than merely listening or reading" does. Rosario Dove, his seventh-grade science teacher, provocatively asked, "What makes you think that?" Dr. Martin smiled and answered, "Everyone doesn't learn by listening." Mrs. Dove responded with, "Everyone doesn't learn by working in small groups either." Dr. Martin nodded. "You're right. However, those who do learn that way will have a good chance to succeed!"

FOR WHOM, WHEN, AND HOW OFTEN ARE SMALL-GROUP TECHNIQUES APPROPRIATE?

Both the principal and the teacher were correct. Analytic, auditory, authority-oriented students learn best from conventional teachers, but peer-oriented youngsters often learn better with classmates—particularly those whom they like. Many learning-style variables contribute to how each person learns and remembers new and difficult information and skills.

Dependent on the age of the population, approximately 20% of middle school and high-school students profit substantially from direct-teacher instruction, and about 28% learn well with peers, but most of those learn best in *pairs* rather than in teams of four or more. More highly achieving youngsters tend to learn well independently, and many others appreciate variety—sometimes learning in a small group, sometimes in a pair, sometimes alone, and sometimes with their teacher. How this last group learns best usually *depends on their interest in what is being taught* or how well they like the classmates with whom they are *teamed.* Using small-group techniques two or three times each week is likely to increase many students' interest and complement different learning styles periodically. But that is not as effective as saying to the class, "You may do this assignment alone if you wish, or work with one or two classmates. Or you may carry your chair quietly to this section of the room where you can work near me." After students have experienced all three instructional formations, they will *know* which works best for them individually.

TEAM LEARNING TO INTRODUCE NEW AND DIFFICULT CONTENT

One of the more effective approaches to introducing complex and challenging material is a small-group technique called *Team Learning*. Team Learning is particularly effective for *introducing* new and difficult academic material to peer-oriented students who gradually become enthusiastic, motivated, and able to work collegially with classmates. Because this strategy leads to both group and individual recognition, it becomes an enjoyable experience for many youngsters when not used too often. Unfortunately, teachers often overuse small-group strategies or require that everyone in the class engages in them—even those who learn better in alternate approaches. When that occurs, children learn, but they do not enjoy the process and do not retain the comprehensive information easily.

Designing a Team Learning

Begin the process by either writing original material to teach a single new and difficult objective or by adapting sections from a commercial source, such as a textbook or the Internet, that teaches what you want the students to learn. Students should be able to read, understand, and discuss the article, cartoon, material, newspaper clipping, poem, or set of diagrams related to the information that the Team Learning presents.

At the end of the printed material, list a series of at least three (3) different types of questions that should be answered by each group.

- The first type of question should be *factual*—directly related to the reading at the top of the Team Learning page. Whatever you want your students to learn about this topic should be taught in a short series of small sentences or paragraphs. However, this is a *lesson—not a unit*; do not make the reading too long. In fact, the first time you introduce Team Learning, keep the material relatively short—perhaps three paragraphs, so that children can learn from the experience and not be overwhelmed.

- The second type of question on the same Team Learning should be *inferential*—one or more for which readers need to *think* and for which there is no definitively correct answer.
- The third task should require a *creative application of what was learned*—one in which the readers apply what they have learned in the Team Learning reading by making something original, such as a crossword puzzle, a poem, a set of Task Cards, a sculpture, a skit, a song, a timeline, and so forth, that explains the concept.

Next, divide those students who do not want to work independently, or in a pair, into small groups of three to no more than four students each. Each student in the group needs to read the printed material. The group can decide if its members want to read silently or quietly aloud so that everyone in that team hears what is written in the printed matter. Then determine who will serve as each team's recorder (the note-taker). It does not matter how you choose the recorder as long as you stipulate criteria that cannot represent more than one student in each team (to avoid arguments and delays). For example, choose the recorder objectively by saying, "The recorder will be the person with the most pets," or "the one with the longest hair," or "the person whose birthday is closest to October 24th." Avoid any designation that might embarrass anyone such as heaviest, skinniest, shortest, wearing jeans with the most holes, and so forth.

Allocate the time interval that students have in which to read the printed information and answer all the questions you have posed (perhaps 20–25 minutes). Explain that everyone should discuss each answer but that

- only the recorder may write;
- the recorder writes only the *team-agreed-upon answers* (not his own);
- the recorder must ask each person, "Do you agree?" Only an answer to which the entire team agrees can be adopted by the team and written by the recorder.
- In the event that someone on the team supports a different answer, that member may write his/her own. (Of course, the team may decide that the second answer better represents its view and then change its answer, which means that the recorder then may write the changed team answer.)

When you notice that most of the groups have answered the Team Learning exercise and completed the creative task, stop the discussion and ask everyone present to cease discussion and come to order. Read aloud the first question you assigned to the Team Learning and call on volunteering students to provide an answer. Briefly display each answer on the chalk- or whiteboard, an overhead, or on a computer so that students can see the correct spelling of each response and copy it if they wish to do so. Ask for other answers, and clarify responses.

Then ask the second question in the Team Learning and call on volunteering students to provide their team's answer. Ask for other possible responses. Indicate the answers that are correct. Continue through all the factual questions. Then call on each team to provide its answers to the inferential questions by discussing possible alternative responses with the class. After that, have each team share its creative product. Accord respect to each endeavor, but emphasize that the task must respond to the objective on which it is based. All students, including the recorder, actively participate.

Teacher's Guide for Using a Team Learning

Depending on the grade level and topic, questions can range from fairly easy to solve (for the first factual question) to relatively difficult ones even for students who have been at the head of their class. Working in small groups can help students become able to provide answers; having discussed (and agreed upon) them beforehand, most should be able to participate well enough. Below are samples of a couple of Team Learning exercises at different levels.

Sample Team Learning for Young Children: Team Learning on Vegetables

Step 1: Develop a set of two-part Task Cards each with a picture of a vegetable on one half of the front and that same vegetable's name on the other half of the front side. Also develop a set of Task Cards with a picture of a fruit on one half of the front and that same fruit's name on the other half of the front side.

Step 2: Place a mixture of fruit and vegetable Task Cards with each team—either individuals, pairs, or a team of three. Say to the children:

"Vegetables and fruits are both foods. Carefully look at the Task Cards in front of your team and decide which are vegetables and which are fruits. Place all the vegetables into one pile and all the fruits into another pile. Your team has four minutes to decide which are the vegetables and which are the fruits."

Step 3: Look at all the vegetable and fruit pictures on the Task Cards. Name any two vegetables and any two fruits that are NOT pictured on the Task Cards.

Step 4. Draw a picture of one vegetable and one fruit that are NOT on the Task Cards or print the first letter in that vegetable's and fruit's name.

Team Learning on the Three Branches of Government

Principal Roger Bloom created this Team Learning for his middle-school adolescents. By allowing students to learn the information independently, in pairs, or in small groups of three or four, he permitted sociological choices, provided a bit of variety, and allowed them to learn by reading the text (visual text), seeing the illustrations (visual picture), discussing (verbal), taking notes based on the discussion (tactual and auditory), and sitting (or standing or kneeling) comfortably.

TEAM LEARNING

Team Members:
1. ______________________ 3. ______________________
2. ______________________ 4. ______________________
Recorder: ______________________

Directions: Read the poem entitled "CHECKING Out the Performance" and answer the questions that follow by reaching a consensus.

CHECKING Out the Performance
By Roger Bloom

One warm summer day theater-goers stood in order
To see a new show performed south of the border.
People held tickets tightly in hand,
As musicians marched by in a big brass band.
Someone called out, "Which show will you see?"
And the response was, "The Family Tree of Liberty!"
The passerby shouted, "I know not of that show."
The response came with a fiery glow: "The Executive, Legislative, and Judicial branches—roles every patriot should know!"

A large man opened the theater doors,
The crowd entered in rows of fours.
Each person received a program 'bout the play,
Many folks shouted, "This will be a great day!"

People quietly found their seats,
As the orchestra played drum-roll beats.
The theater lights began to dim,
And a man appeared who was very slim.

"Welcome to the Family Tree of Liberty,
This is a marvelous spectacle to see.
Sit back, relax, and enjoy the show,
Let's travel back to the 1770s of long ago."
As the man left the stage to the right,
The curtains burst open with a red, white, and blue light.
The orchestra's music began to play,
On stage were the founding fathers with much to say.

"Welcome to the city of Boston," said Sam Adams with a smile,
"Meet England's King George, who is worse than vile.
He taxed us on stamps, sugar, shipping, and tea,
In defense we formed the Sons of Liberty.
Taxes without representation took us by surprise,
We thirteen colonies broke away from the man we despise."
Enter Thomas Jefferson, one of the greatest authors of our times,
He penned the Declaration of Independence and told of King George's crimes.

Jefferson said, "We have had enough abusive power,
We must break away from England's ivory tower."
The Declaration of Independence created a unified state
In 1776—remember that date!
As Jefferson exited who was next to appear?
The great George Washington whom we all revere!
His troops died in Yorktown in the Revolutionary War
To form the United States and shove King George out the door!

They died to create a nation of women and men
With a government no king could abuse ever again.
Washington asked the Constitutional Convention delegates to join the mix,
He pleaded, "Our troops built our nation with constitutional bricks.
Our troops feared abuse and what tyranny could bring, and
Created a government where freedom bells ring!"
Those delegates created a system of checks and balances then
So that no branch could ever be all-powerful again.
James Madison walked on stage, and said to everyone there,

"Creating checks and balances was the greatest idea!
We created that system to take no chances,

To ensure equality among the three branches.
The time has come to protect ourselves from corruption,
And assure that our government avoids destruction."

Madison urged Washington to ride to Philadelphia that day
To explain how three branches could protect us in every way.
The Executive branch has the power to check what the Legislative branch wills,
The President's days are consumed with vetoing bills.
The Executive branch has the power to check what the Judicial branch construes
By nominating justices and judges, and pardoning a few.

Madison added, "The Legislative branch has power to check the Executive as well,
It approves of treaties, nominates, and overrides vetoes—a lot to do!
The Legislative branch can check the Judicial branch too.
It confirms justices and judges—definitive power that's true.
The Judicial branch checks the other two—to preserve liberty
With the power to declare laws and actions unconstitutional—to protect you and me."

After Madison's explanation was made loud and clear,
Sam Adams and Tom Jefferson had more thoughts to share.
Adams said, "Mr. Washington and Mr. Madison, you are masters at creation,
To devise a system of checks and balances—it fills me with elation."
Jefferson added, "The government will be protected from abusive power,
Never will a tyrannical king rule the United States from an ivory tower."
As the curtains closed at the end of the play,
A round of applause echoed all through the day.

Theater-goers loved the show and now knew,
Why a system of checks and balances was "red, white, and blue."
A balance of power is as American as can be
It keeps us safe as a democracy.
It prevents each branch from amassing too much power
And keeps us safe day by day, hour by hour.

1. What are the three branches of government?
2. Who drafted the Declaration of Independence?
3. What is the role of the President?
4. What is the role of the Congress?
5. Whose job is it to do the confirmation of justices and judges?
6. What are checks and balances?
7. Who is the "audience" of the show?
8. Create a poster that illustrates the concept of the "three branches of government."

Or

Create Task Cards highlighting the concept of the "three branches of government."

Or

Create Pic-A-Hole cards highlighting the concept of the "three branches of government."

9. Why did the framers of the Constitution create a government composed of three equal branches?

CIRCLE OF KNOWLEDGE TO REINFORCE NEW AND DIFFICULT CONTENT

To reinforce what has been taught in the Team Learning, use another small-group technique called a Circle of Knowledge (Dunn & Dunn, 1992, 1993, 1999).

Designing a Circle of Knowledge

Circle of Knowledge is one of the best strategies for reviewing something previously taught and is ideal for reinforcing either reading or math knowledge or skills. This technique is highly motivating, competitive, and team based. In an interesting way, it reviews and focuses on one major concept or skill at a time; fosters group effort and individual responses; develops ingenuity in aiding all students to contribute; and eliminates the boredom that usually accompanies repetitive review. It also highlights the talents of those few students who can act, draw, or mimic well.

Step 1: Divide the class into several small circles of three to four chairs or desks in various sections of the room as far from each other as possible.

Step 2: Be certain that each Circle has one large piece of lined paper and a pencil or two.

Step 3: Pose a single question concerning what the class learned during the previous day, week, or month. The questions must generate many possible correct answers, such as: "List all the synonyms you can think of for the word *loyalty*," or "Name all the antonyms you can think of for the word *truthful*," "List all the figures of speech you can," "List all the metaphors you can remember," "Name all the characters in (a specific story or novel)," "List all the facts you can recall about *troubadours,*" "List all the facts you can about haiku poetry," or "Name all the number combinations in which, if you add two numbers together and take away a third number, the answer is 9," and so forth.

Step 4: Now add an unusual amount of time to that incomplete sentence. Circles of Knowledge are always short, so you might add: "in two and ¼ minutes" or "in 3 and 4/5 minutes." You arbitrarily decide how much time you are allotting for this review.

Step 5: Explain that once the single question has been posed, the person sitting to the *right* of the recorder must whisper the first answer to that question to the members of the Circle. The recorder immediately writes the answer that was whispered onto the pad. (Spelling does not count.) Direct the recorders to print the answers clearly so that every one in this Circle can see what is written as each student whispers his or her next answer. The Circle proceeds with each member, in turn, adding one answer. When it is the recorder's turn, he or she also must contribute an answer to the pad.

Step 6: The Circle continues for as many rounds as possible, in which each person contributes one answer per turn during each round. Only one answer is accepted from each student until his or her turn comes around again. Answers are whispered because any Circle member who hears an answer from another Circle "may take it" and add it to their pad. This attempt at secrecy keeps the groups focused and aids in discipline and control.

Step 7: Participants are not permitted to help another member in the same Circle directly if it is that student's turn and he or she can't think of another response. However, the more answers each Circle accumulates, the better chance it has to win the Circle of Knowledge Contest. Thus, anyone in the same Circle may draw, pantomime, or use hand motions or other nonverbal clues—but not write an answer—to help that participant think of another response. If the person cannot add to the number of answers despite assistance, then that Circle must stop and can no longer compete. It is here that the student who can act, draw, or pantomime well becomes a definite asset to his classmates.

Step 8: On the whiteboard, chalkboard, or an overhead projector, horizontally write Circle One, Circle Two, Circle Three, and so on—including a listing for each group.

Step 9: When the allotted amount of time has passed, call "Time" and begin to solicit and record one answer, in turn, from each Circle. Any member of the Circle can call out an answer, but that answer has to have been in writing on that Circle's pad.

Step 10: Call on one Circle in turn after another until each Circle has had a chance to give one answer. For equity, the last group calls out two answers and the sequence reverts until each team has called out its second answer. Thus, for the first round, call on Circles One through Six; then call on

Circles Six through One in reverse order. Then Circle One will call out two answers, and the process continues in this pattern until all Circles have no more answers to give and call out "Pass!"

Step 11: Print every answer that is called out onto the board. If a Circle calls out an incorrect answer, you write it and keep going with no hint to the class that the response is wrong. If any Circle realizes that the answer is incorrect, any of its members may call out, "Challenge!" Turn to the first student whom you hear call out "Challenge" and ask, "Why are you challenging?" If the answer was incorrect, the Circle that called out the challenge gains one point for correctly challenging and the Circle whose member gave the incorrect answer loses one point.

Step 12: No Circle may repeat an answer that already has been given. If an answer is called out and has already been written on the board, anyone in any Circle who hears that repetition being offered may call out "Challenge!" Turn to the first student whom you hear call out "Challenge" and ask, "Why are you challenging?" If the answer is that it already is on the board and therefore is a repeat, the Circle that called out the repetition loses one point from its total score and the Circle that correctly challenged earns one extra point. If any Circle accuses you of calling on another rather than it, repeat, "I call on the first person I *hear*! Challenge more loudly and clearly."

Step 13: Each Circle recorder should cross out any answer that already has been given from its own game pad, but should add any answers that the Circle did not have but may have been correctly given by another player. New correct answers may be added to the recorder's list so that the Circle sees information that may have been overlooked. However, after that particular answer has been tallied on the board, it is a good idea to cross it off so that no one inadvertently calls it out again—causing the Circle to lose another point.

Step 14: If any challenge is incorrect, the Circle that gave it has one point deducted from its score.

Sample Circles of Knowledge

Sample Circles of Knowledge for primary-school children:

- List all the words you can think of that start with the letter *B*. (2½ minutes)
- Name all the words that you can that include a "long *A*" sound. (3½ minutes)
- List all the boys' names that begin with the letter *R*. (3⅕ minutes)

- List all the compound words that you can. ($3\frac{1}{6}$ minutes)
- List all the words you can that rhyme with *at*. ($2\frac{1}{9}$ minutes)

Sample Circles of Knowledge for elementary-school children:

- List as many adverbs as you can. (2½ minutes)
- List all the synonyms you can for the word *small*. ($4\frac{1}{10}$ minutes)
- Write all the words you know that are related to the circus. (3½ minutes)
- Name all the punctuation marks you know. (2 minutes)
- Write all the spelling words you remember that included more than six letters. (3½ minutes)
- List all the reasons why we should help non-English-speaking children learn to speak English. ($2\frac{1}{8}$ minutes)
- List all the reasons why everyone should learn to speak other languages. ($2\frac{3}{5}$ minutes)

Sample Circles of Knowledge for middle-school students: (4½ minutes each)

- List all the rules you can remember for writing a correct business letter.
- Name as many American plays as you can.
- List the titles of all the books you ever read about famous people.
- Name as many American poets as you can.
- Develop as many analogies as you can.
- List all the natural forces that have changed the surface of our planet.
- List all the reasons why we never should "put anyone down" verbally.

To accompany the Team Learning he developed on *"Checking" Out the Performance*, Mr. Bloom designed this Circle of Knowledge.

Circle Members:
1. ______________________ 3. ______________________
2. ______________________ 4. ______________________
Recorder: ______________________

List the ways in which our system of checks and balances has prevented one branch of the United States government from becoming more powerful than the others.

GROUP ANALYSIS

Most schooling favors reflective learners—those who think long and hard about the question they're asked and the answer they want to give. Reflective learners need to repeat the question to themselves before they actually seek an answer. They then explore the possible answers that come to mind and need to be certain that theirs is correct before they can call it out.

Impulsive learners are very different from their reflective counterparts. They call out because they think they know the answer (and often do) but do not raise their hands to be called on or wait their turns. Teachers invariably discourage impulsive learners in the effort to maintain control of the knowledge flow and student behaviors.

Group Analysis is a small-group technique that favors impulsive learners. Whereas Team Learning and Circle of Knowledge require disciplined thinking (maintaining the proper sequence, specifically answering each objective, remembering certain information, and so forth), Group Analysis encourages spontaneity and creativity. There are few restrictions to the line of thinking a child must take, and as long as answers are logical and reasonable, there is nothing "right" or "wrong." In this way, Group Analysis may be one of the few strategies teachers employ that level the playing field for their impulsive thinkers.

Designing a Group Analysis

There are many strategies for designing a Group Analysis, but one that takes virtually no time or preparation is to find any large painting, photo, or picture. A cartoon will do, as will an unusual costume or prop. Merely have everyone sit (or stand) quietly with their attention toward the item you have brought to class covered with a bath towel, sheet, or thick plastic that cannot be seen through. Tell the class one line that vaguely suggests their task, such as, "The item under this cover might be used for any number of tasks. Imagine what it possibly could do, and then write your ideas in a word or two on a sheet of paper."

Theorizing or philosophizing is not a skill children ordinarily are encouraged to develop—although they should. This activity takes exactly the amount of time you are willing to devote to it, but it will stretch students' imagination and thinking and open their horizons to multiple possibilities. Try it! See what happens. Also watch to see how difficult many reflectives find this task and how well impulsives perform under this new set of circumstances.

Rush Hour in New York City. *Courtesy of Rosette Allegretti*

Group Members:
1. ______________________ 3. ______________________
2. ______________________ 4. ______________________
Recorder: ______________________

What's the Rush? Group Analysis

Directions: Look at the photo entitled *Rush Hour in New York City* on the previous page. In your group, discuss ways to improve rush hour traffic in big cities.

Sample Group Analysis Tasks

1. As a group, have students look at an intriguing photograph you selected from a website such as www.nationalgeographic.com or www.timeforkids.com. Have them describe what they think is occurring in the picture.
2. Using a series of two to four photographs or clip art images, have students establish a logical connection among the pictures.
3. Using photographs of children taken in your school, have students guess where these children are and what they are doing.

Textbox 7.1. Where Do Small Group Techniques Fit into the Learning-Styles Implementation Process?

STAGE 1

Learning-Styles Assessment
(See www.learningstyles.net for LS assessment tools)

- Share information with students, parents, all teachers.
- Help students use LS profiles and study guides to become self-directed learners.
- Raise awareness about time-of-day energy levels.
- Make adaptations for global vs. analytic teaching.

STAGE 2

Initial Implementation Steps

- Environmental accommodations (Room redesign)
- Methodologies and resources to respond to perceptual preferences
- *Small-group instructional techniques*

GRAPHIC GUIDE TO IMPLEMENTATION OF SMALL-GROUP TECHNIQUES

Experimenting with small-group instructional techniques will prove to be an enjoyable, familiar task to most teachers. Those who tried pair work or cooperative learning will appreciate the ease with which these activities can be implemented along with or independent of all other learning-style techniques (see textbox 7.1).

REFLECTION POINTS

1. Design and implement at least one Team Learning, Circle of Knowledge, and Group Analysis activity with your students. Share your experiences with fellow teachers and ask for feedback on the activities.
2. Compare and contrast select cooperative-learning techniques you have tried with the small-group techniques introduced in this chapter. In which ways do Team Learning, Circle of Knowledge, and Group Analysis support at-risk students' learning needs?

Chapter Eight

Teaching At-Risk Students with Contract Activity Packages

Mrs. Morrison printed the class assignment on the board with specific directions. "Read pages 178–205 and answer all the end-of-chapter questions by developing one of the following activities:

1. a crossword puzzle;
2. a rhyming poem;
3. a rap; or
4. a large Flip Chute with an accompanying set of cards.

You may do the assignment alone, in a pair, or in a group of three."

Many students began by copying the assignment into their notebooks. Some read it first and then set right to work. Others questioned classmates for clarification. Tenika Jones immediately challenged Mrs. Morrison. "We four want to work together. Why can't we?" The teacher smiled and answered, "Actually you *can*, but if four of you are creating one Activity Alternative, it has to be better than any project developed by any individual or pair."

"That's not fair!" Tenika responded. "That's the rule," the teacher answered. Tenika and her friends considered that statement and decided to work in two pairs.

In the meantime, most students became busily engaged. Anthony had another question. "I'd like to answer the questions by creating a podcast on the computer. I don't like those other choices much." "Go to it!" Mrs. Morrison encouraged her young computer whiz! Students settled into a variety of readings, discussions, and activities. Everyone seemed engaged as the teacher walked about asking and answering queries.

LEARNING-STYLE CHARACTERISTICS THAT RESPOND TO CONTRACT ACTIVITY PACKAGES

Two distinctly different types of students—often with different learning-style traits—fare very well with a Contract Activity Package (CAP). The first type is a motivated auditory and visual learner who is task persistent. Such youth tend to be independent and achieving. The second type is an auditory and/or visual learner who may be nonconforming and challenging. Some of these youth are behavioral problems—and as such, may become students at risk of academic failure—*until* they have the opportunity to learn through a CAP. Then, they often transition into more focused and more motivated learners.

CONTRACT ACTIVITY PACKAGES: ONE APPROACH TO LEARNING

A CAP is an instructional method that allows motivated persons to learn at their own speed. A CAP consists of several components:

- clearly stated *Objectives*;
- *Alternative Resources* that permit choices of multisensory materials to complement individuals' perceptual preferences;
- Activity Alternatives in which students use new information or skills by creating an original resource that shows that they did learn what was required;
- *Reporting Alternatives* encourage a sharing of each students' original Activity Alternative with classmates who are studying the same material;
- at least three different *Small-Group Techniques* to permit students who enjoy working or learning with classmates to do so. These usually include at least one Team Learning, one Circle of Knowledge, and/or Brainstorming, Case Study, Group Analysis, or Role Playing. It is permissible to include more than one Team Learning and Circle of Knowledge as long as at least three different techniques are required;
- an objectives-based *Assessment* at the end of the CAP directly related to whatever the students are required to learn. This assessment evaluates how much has been learned and may include students' performances, portfolios, projects, or written work.

CAPs accommodate a variety of learning-style characteristics such as sound, light, temperature, seating design, choices versus required tasks, social preferences, perceptual strengths, intake, time of day, and mobility needs. They provide structure through the itemization of specific Objectives, Activity and Reporting Alternatives, Small-Group Techniques, and directly related Self-Assessments. They provide options through the choice of some Objectives, some Activity and Reporting Alternatives, the resources they may use to master the information, and where in the environment and with whom they may work. By permitting these choices, CAPs provide *breathing room* for nonconformists who often resist direction or structure from authoritative persons—often construed to be the teacher or administrator.

A SAMPLE CONTRACT ACTIVITY PACKAGE

Below is one example of a middle school mini-CAP developed by Honigsfeld (1999) to introduce both this instructional method and the topic at the same time. Many other complete CAPs are available for comparison in Dunn & Dunn, (1992, 1993, 1999; Carbo, Dunn, & Dunn, 1986; Dunn & Blake, 2008) and at www.learningstyles.net listed under Resources. The website has many "matched" Programmed Learning Sequences (see chapter 9) and CAPs available for interested educators and parents.

Global Warming: It's Not Cool!

By the time you finish this Contract Activity Package and complete any four (4) of Objectives 1, 2, 3, 4 and 5, you should know a great deal about global warming and how to protect our Earth from it.

You should be able to:

1. explain what global warming is;
2. list at least three (3) causes of global warming;
3. describe the *greenhouse effect*;
4. make at least three (3) predictions about what might happen if global warming continues; and
5. describe how we can slow down global warming.

Name: ______________________________ Class: _________________
Date started: ______________________________
Test grade: ______________________________
Date completed: ___________________________

If you prefer, you may work on this CAP with one (1) or two (2) other students. If you do, write their names here:

Team member's name: _________________________________
Team member's name: _________________________________

_______________________ ___________________________
Student's signature Teacher's signature

Objective 1. Explain what global warming is.
Please do at least one (1) of the following:

Activity Alternatives	***Reporting Alternatives***
1. Draw a picture or cartoon that shows what global warming is. (V/T)	1. Display your drawing on the bulletin board and ask classmates to comment on it by attaching stick-on notes.
2. Make a set of Flip Chute cards that explain what global warming and related science concepts mean. (T)	2. Have two (2) students use your Flip Chute cards. Ask them to suggest ways of improving them.
3. Create a skit that teaches other children about global warming (K).	3. Present your skit to a small group of students younger than you. Be certain they understand what global warming is.
4. Interview at least three (3) people about global warming. (A/K)	4. Report back to your teacher on what you have learned during your interviews.

Objective 2. List at least three (3) causes of global warming.
Please do at least one (1) of the following:

Activity Alternatives	***Reporting Alternatives***
1. Make up a song that explains what causes global warming. (A)	1. Sing your song to three (3) classmates.

2. Create a collage that shows the causes of global warming. (T/V)	2. Place your collage in the the Science Center. Describe your collage to two (2) friends.
3. Take a walk in your neighborhood. Make a list of causes of global warming "in your own backyard." (K)	3. Share your list with your parents and teacher.
4. Design an Electroboard that teaches about the causes of global warming. (T)	4. Ask two (2) classmates to work with your resource.

Objective 3. Describe the *greenhouse effect.*
Please do at least one (1) of the following:

Activity Alternatives	***Reporting Alternatives***
1. Construct a 3D model to illustrate the greenhouse effect. (T/V)	1. Display your model and answer questions about it.
2. Draw a diagram that shows the three parts of the greenhouse effect. Prepare labels that go with the illustration. (V/T)	2. Ask two (2) students to correctly place labels on the diagram.
3. Visit local botanical gardens. Ask a volunteer to show you how the greenhouse works. Take notes and compare and contrast what you learned in the gardens with what you learned in school about the greenhouse effect. (K)	3. Tell three (3) classmates about your trip. Explain to them the similarities and differences between a greenhouse and the greenhouse effect.
4. Make up riddles about the greenhouse effect. (A)	4. Ask two (2) classmates to solve your riddles.

Objective 4: Make at least three (3) predictions about what might happen if global warming continues.
Please do at least one (1) of the following:

Activity Alternatives	***Reporting Alternatives***
1. Create a newsletter that warns people of the possible dangers of global warming. (V/T)	1. Send your newsletter to at least five (5) people.
2. Make up a story about what might happen if we don't stop global warming. Audio record your story. (A)	2. Have at least three (3) students listen to your recording and comment on it.

3. Design a Floor Game that teaches about the effects of global warming. (K)
4. Make a crossword puzzle that contains at least six (6) words related to the topic of global warming. (T/V)

3. Invite a small group of students to try your game.
4. Ask three (3) classmates to solve your crossword puzzle.

Objective 5: Describe how we can slow down global warming.
Please do at least one (1) of the following:

Activity Alternatives

1. Design a poster that encourages everybody to save our Earth by slowing down global warming (V/T)
2. Send an e-mail message to students in at least two (2) schools in the United States or abroad. In your letter tell them about how you feel about global warming and ask them to share their thoughts with you. (T)
3. Prepare an announcement for the school radio on what everybody in the community can do to help protect the environment and slow down global warming. (A)
4. Pretend you are a member of a team that works on preventing global warming. Make a plan on how to teach children about the environment. (K)

Reporting Alternatives

1. Display your poster in your classroom. Autograph it.
2. Show the responses you receive to your teacher.
3. Ask your teacher's and principal's permission to make the announcement on Earth Day.
4. Ask a friend to join you in the activity. Share your plan with third friend.

BRAINSTORMING

Team Members:
1. ____________________ 3. ____________________
3. ____________________ 4. ____________________
5. ____________________ Recorder

Write a list of rules that people can follow to keep our Earth clean. You have 4 minutes and 44 seconds to do that.

TEAM LEARNING

Team Members:

1. ______________________ 3. ______________________
3. ______________________ 4. ______________________
5. ______________________ Recorder

Read the following paragraphs or listen to the audio recording and discuss the questions with your group. Answer all the questions together. If you do not agree, you may write your own answer.

The Greenhouse Effect

Every day more and more of the rain forests are burned down because people need room to build new cities or to grow plants or to raise animals such as cows or sheep. However, burning the rain forests is dangerous. It adds extra carbon dioxide to the air.

Carbon dioxide is a gas that people and animals breathe out. Scientists believe that more carbon dioxide (CO_2) in the atmosphere will make our Earth warmer. Trees and other green plants take in CO_2 and give off oxygen. You remember, oxygen is part of the air that people and animals need to survive. So, burning the Earth's forests brings *double trouble*. Not only does the burning itself add CO_2 to the atmosphere, but when the trees are gone, they no longer can take the CO_2 from the air or make the oxygen that animals and people need. The more CO_2 in the air, the more heat is trapped in our atmosphere and the warmer our Earth becomes. This is called the *greenhouse effect*. Scientists predict that by the year 2050 most of the world will have warmer weather.

(Adapted from Hoven, L. (1990). *Thematic Unit: Jungle*. Huntington Beach, CA: Teacher Created Materials.)

1. What is burned every day?
2. Why do people burn the rain forests?
3. What does CO_2 stand for?
4. Why is burning a forest double trouble?
5. How does CO_2 make our Earth warmer?
6. Either draw a diagram that illustrates the greenhouse effect on Earth or write a poem describing the greenhouse effect on Earth.

CIRCLE OF KNOWLEDGE

Team Members:

1. ______________________ 3. ______________________
3. ______________________ 4. ______________________
5. ______________________ Recorder

List all the vocabulary words you can think of that are related to the topic of global warming. Be prepared to explain why you included each word in your list. Be certain everyone on your Team knows what each word means. You have 3 minutes and 33 seconds. Good luck!

1. ______________________	11. ______________________
2. ______________________	12. ______________________
3. ______________________	13. ______________________
4. ______________________	14. ______________________
5. ______________________	15. ______________________
6. ______________________	16. ______________________
7. ______________________	17. ______________________
8. ______________________	18. ______________________
9. ______________________	19. ______________________
10. ______________________	20. ______________________

Unit Test

Answer at least four (4) of the following five (5) questions. If you answer all five questions correctly, you will be my expert assistant in designing the next science CAP.

1. What is global warming? Give a 2–3 sentence explanation.
2. Circle the causes of global warming:
   - Summers are longer than winters.
   - Cars and factories pollute the air.
   - People don't recycle everything they should.
   - Forests are cut down.
   - Certain gases in our planet's atmosphere trap heat.
   - The Earth is getting closer to the sun.
3. Create a diagram below to explain the greenhouse effect.
4. What could happen if we don't stop global warming?
   Write T (true) or F (false) in front of each statement:

_______ 1. We won't have winters any more.
_______ 2. The polar ice caps will melt.
_______ 3. The sea level will rise.
_______ 4. Cities on the coast will be flooded.
_______ 5. Summers will be very hot and dry.
_______ 6. Solar energy will be wasted.

5. What can be done to prevent global warming? Answer in 2–3 sentences. You may also illustrate your answer.

Resource Alternatives

Books:

Cherry, L., & Braasch, G. (2008). *How we know what we know about our changing climate: Scientists and kids explore global warming*. Nevada City, CA: Dawn.

Gore, A. (2006). *An inconvenient truth: The planetary emergency of global warming and what we can do about it*. New York: Rodale.

Gore, A. (2007). *An inconvenient truth: The crisis of global warming*. New York: Penguin Young Readers Group.

Dashefsky, H. S. (1995). *Kids can make a difference: Environmental science activities*. New York: TAB Books.

Kaufman, D. G. (1996). *Hands-on environmental education activities for K–6*. Dubuque, IA: Kendall/Hunt.

MacEachern, D. (1990). *Save our planet—750 everyday ways you can help clean up the Earth*. New York: Dell.

David, L., & Gordon, C. (2007). *The down-to-earth guide to global warming*. New York: Scholastic.

De Rothschild, D., Reiner, R., Wall, K., & Van Roden, W. (2007). *The live Earth global warming survival handbook*. New York: Rodale.

Johnson, K. D., & Bonnell, M. A. (2007). *Gas trees and car turds: A kid's guide to the roots of global warming*. Golden, CO: Fulcrum.

Murphy, G. (2008). *A kid's guide to global warming*. New York: Barnes and Noble.

Thornhill, J. (2007). *This is my planet: A kid's guide to global warming*. Ontario, Canada: Maple Tree Press.

Video Cassettes/DVDs:

An Inconvenient Truth DVD (2006)
Arctic Tale DVD (2007)
Global Warming: The Signs and the Science. PBS Video. (2006)
Planet Earth: Global Warming (2007)

Multisensory Resources:

Global Warming: Programmed Learning Sequence
Global Warming: Flip Chute
Race to Save the Earth: Floor Game

The Greenhouse Effect: Task Cards
What Causes Global Warming? Electroboard

Internet Resources:
http://globalwarmingkids.net/
http://epa.gov/climatechange/kids/gw.html
http://www.pewclimate.org/global-warming-basics/kidspage.cfm
http://www.timeforkids.com/TFK/specials/articles/0,6709,1113542,00.html
http://kids.nationalgeographic.com

DIFFERENTIATING CAPS

The sample CAP on Global Warming was designed for upper elementary or lower middle school grades. It was field-tested both with third and sixth graders in the New York City public school system. The difficulty level and the complexity of this CAP can be adjusted both for lower elementary grades or high school students. Three objectives would be sufficient for a second-grade class, whereas middle schoolers can tackle six to eight objectives or more.

How to Make a CAP More Accessible for At-Risk Students

- Reduce the number of objectives and simplify their content.
- Shorten the small-group techniques.
- Assign Activity and Reporting Alternatives that are age appropriate and complement your students' cognitive abilities.
- Reduce the number and type of resources available for students, but definitely include several tactual resources and Floor or Wall Games.
- Scaffold the assessment (offer partially completed answers and sentence starters).
- Simplify the language and content of the entire CAP.

How to Make a CAP More Challenging

- Increase the number of objectives and their level of difficulty.
- Expand on and extend the small-group techniques.
- Create more thought-provoking Activity and Reporting Alternatives.
- Encourage the selection of independent resources on the topic in addition to those you compiled for the students.
- Create an assessment component that either resembles standardized tests or requires creative applications.
- Enhance both the language and content of the entire CAP.

ASSESSING STUDENT PERFORMANCE

A Contract Activity Package allows for both formative (ongoing) and summative (final) assessments. As students either independently or in small groups complete various tasks, their performance on each informs both the learner and the teacher about content attainment and provides feedback on the teaching-learning process to both. The CAP Unit Test serves as the final formal assessment that measures the degree to which the student met the objectives.

A CAP also provides a framework for two types of student performance—individual and group. The first type of assessment is inherently embedded in the Reporting Alternatives that require students to share the creative resources each developed—an accomplishment that simultaneously reinforces for classmates what was studied, but with an interesting alternative product. The ultimate goal for all students is to master the objectives, but each could take a different avenue to get there. The reporting can be done both formally and informally. Thus, the assessment data gained also may be formal or informal.

The second type of assessment is incorporated into the small-group techniques, such as Brainstorming (ideal for preassessment), Team Learning (ongoing assessment), and Circle of Knowledge (to be used toward the completion of the unit). Flexible grouping structures throughout the CAP's small-group techniques allow students to work with different classmates and receive feedback from a variety of peers.

GRAPHIC GUIDE TO THE IMPLEMENTATION OF CONTRACT ACTIVITY PACKAGES

If you want to know where in the process CAPs fit, they tend to be implemented in the following sequence—although you certainly could try using a CAP with auditorily and visually motivated students, or with those who may be nonconforming, without using other learning-style strategies (see textbox 8.1).

REFLECTION POINTS

1. Review the chapter-opening vignette. Experiment with Activity Alternatives and Reporting Alternatives on a small scale first. Identify an upcoming unit you will be teaching and design Activity and Reporting Alternatives for students' homework assignments at the end of each lesson.

Textbox 8.1. Where Do CAPs Fit into the Learning-Styles Implementation Process?

STAGE 1

Learning-Styles Assessment
(See www.learningstyles.net for LS assessment tools)

- Share information with students, parents, all teachers.
- Help students use LS profiles and study guides to become self-directed learners.
- Raise awareness about time-of-day energy levels.
- Make adaptations for global vs. analytic teaching.

STAGE 2

Initial Implementation Steps

- Environmental accommodations (Room redesign)
- Methodologies and resources to respond to perceptual preferences
- Small-group instructional techniques

STAGE 3

Advanced Implementation Steps

- *Contract Activity Packages*

2. The CAP may be a "contract" agreed to by the individual student and teacher, but need not be so formal. Consider parental involvement if you are so disposed, and develop ways to include parents both in the contract and the learning process if that seems warranted.
3. Revise the sample CAP on global warming to alert students to our planetary crisis and match their needs by simplifying or enhancing it based on the guidelines above.

Chapter Nine

Teaching Visual/Tactual Students Who Need Structure with Programmed Learning Sequences

Have you ever seriously thought about how at-risk students actually learn? Is their progress steady and predictable? If you had to submit an overview of how they master new and difficult content, would you say that they remember some information easily but grapple with other content at other times? Do they often take "two steps forward and one step back"? Do they find it difficult to "stay on task"? Do they have "short attention spans"?

Let's consider a student with whom we worked recently. To date, Johanna has not been referred to Special Education because she has no identified learning disability. However, the Child Study Team that repeatedly discussed her case believes that she has unaddressed problems and assigned her to Academic Intervention Service (AIS) classes. Johanna's classroom and AIS teachers agree that she probably requires a very structured instructional environment in which each task and assignment is carefully planned and explained to her. They believe that if Johanna's entire school day could be divided into well-managed, shorter time spans with specific activities, she might be able to progress. For such a plan to be effective, Johanna would need predictable patterns so that each activity follows the previous one in a highly scheduled day. Also, because her reading skills are somewhat limited, Johanna probably needs someone (an aide, a classmate, or an older student) to read the text when she encounters challenging vocabulary.

Without knowing Johanna's learning style, how could the Child Study Team members be certain that their diagnosis is correct? After all, Johanna might need some structure, but she also might:

- tire of it if her learning-style profile also indicates that she likes to learn with peers (as many poor achievers do). In that event, Team Learning would be the first strategy to use.

- need periodic variety if she quickly becomes bored with a single structured strategy.
- yearn for some choice. In that case, we might consider a Contract Activity Package.
- be highly tactual. If that were correct, our first choice would be a Programmed Learning Sequence.

What would we need to know in addition to the fact that Johanna performs better with than without structure? The next item we would seek would be her perceptual strength.

If Johanna were auditory, she might perform best with recorded books. If she were visual, she also would respond to a need for structure and either visual print or visual pictures. If she were tactual, we'd recommend a Programmed Learning Sequence, for that approach offers a combination of structured visual print, visual picture, and tactual components and, in addition, a recording for slow readers and periodic tactual supplements.

WHAT IS A PROGRAMMED LEARNING SEQUENCE?

One very effective instructional strategy for students like Johanna is a Programmed Learning Sequence (PLS)—an approach similar to an illustrated, interactive storybook based on the required subject matter. A PLS begins globally as a story and is structured so that learning occurs in small increments and is reinforced periodically with an interesting, game-like tactual resource. An accompanying audio recording allows students to follow along independently or with a peer. If a PLS is designed on the computer, sound can be added to the frames digitally.

CHARACTERISTICS OF STUDENTS FOR WHOM PROGRAMMED LEARNING SEQUENCES WORK

A PLS is for students whose learning styles indicate a preference for structure, visual text and picture input, and tactual stimulation. An engaging introductory story or anecdote captures the attention of global processors, whereas its step-by-step approach to learning new and difficult information appeals to those who process information analytically. The audio component of the PLS supports struggling readers by adding sensory input or enhances the experience for auditory learners who prefer to listen to new information in the first place.

DESCRIPTION OF PROGRAMMED LEARNING SEQUENCES

If you want to experiment with a PLS for students who are likely to perform well with this structured, visual/tactual resource, follow these directions. First, decide on a unit of study you need to teach, establish age-appropriate objectives, and create an illustrated storybook about the content by including the following key elements:

1. a colorful, eye-catching cover in a shape related to the topic of the PLS, to which both visual and tactual learners will respond;
2. a global introduction, perhaps a story that runs through the entire PLS;
3. clearly stated objectives;
4. a succinct explanation of how to use the PLS;
5. a vocabulary frame introducing new and difficult words in print and with illustrations of each word;
6. a series of *frames* (pages) that contain colorful, appropriate graphics;
7. mini tactual-review frames inserted every five to seven frames to reinforce learning through an Electroboard, Task Cards, a Wrap Around, or Pic-A-Hole (see chapter 5 on tactual materials) attached to a separate frame;
8. illustrations related to the topic throughout the PLS;
9. on the back of each frame, where the answers to the questions on the previous frame are inserted, a humorous statement or teasing related to the answer or topic to keep global students' attention;
10. a final assessment, such as a unit test; and
11. a reminder to erase answers for the next student who uses the PLS.

A SAMPLE PROGRAMMED LEARNING SEQUENCE DESIGNED FOR AT-RISK STUDENTS

Below is one example of a mini-PLS to illustrate the content and format. Figure 9.1 is a revised, slightly abbreviated version of the original PLS specifically designed for either upper-elementary or lower–middle school at-risk students as either a regular or supplementary science unit on global warming (Honigsfeld, 1999). In Chapter 8, you saw how a Contract Activity Package addresses these identical objectives. The colorful, brightly illustrated, laminated PLS has been recreated here to illustrate the scope and sequence of the material presented to students in grades three through six on the topic of global warming.

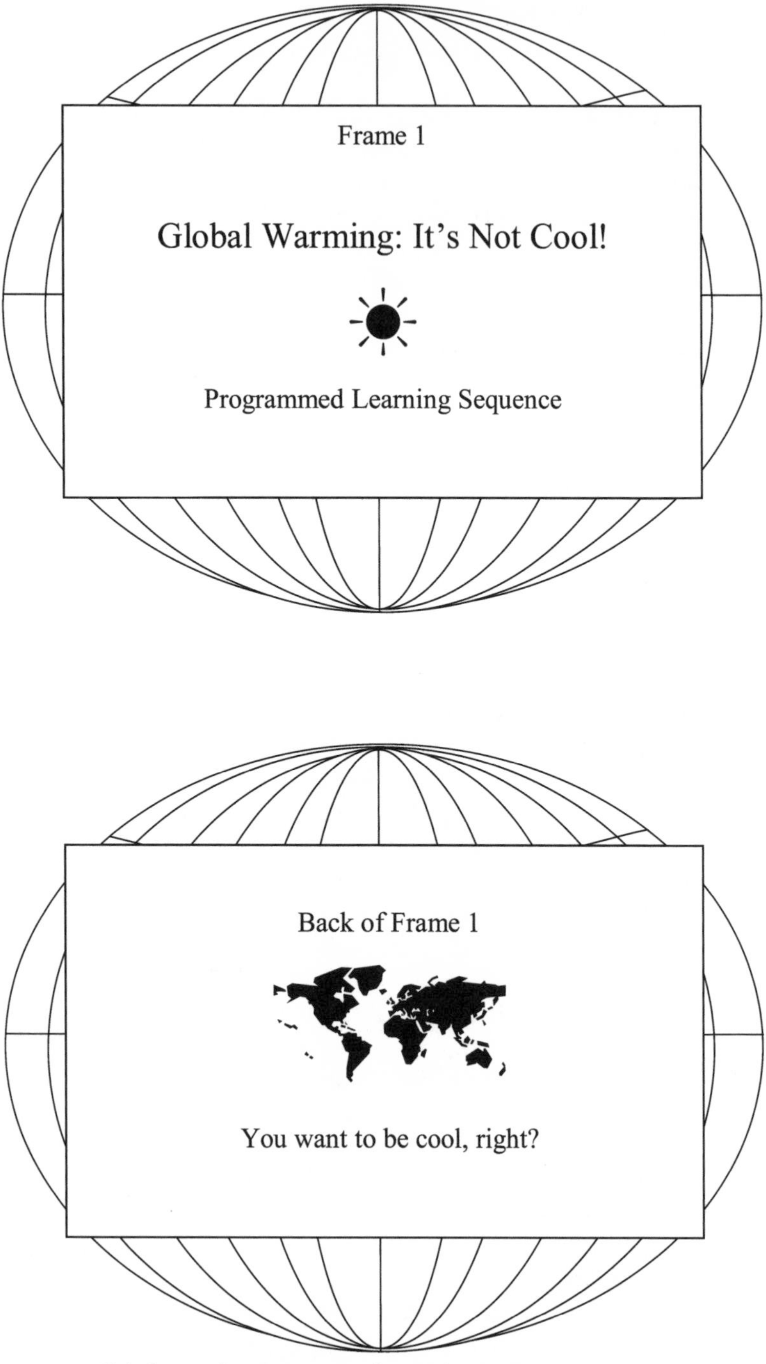

Figure 9.1. Global Warming Programmed Learning Sequence

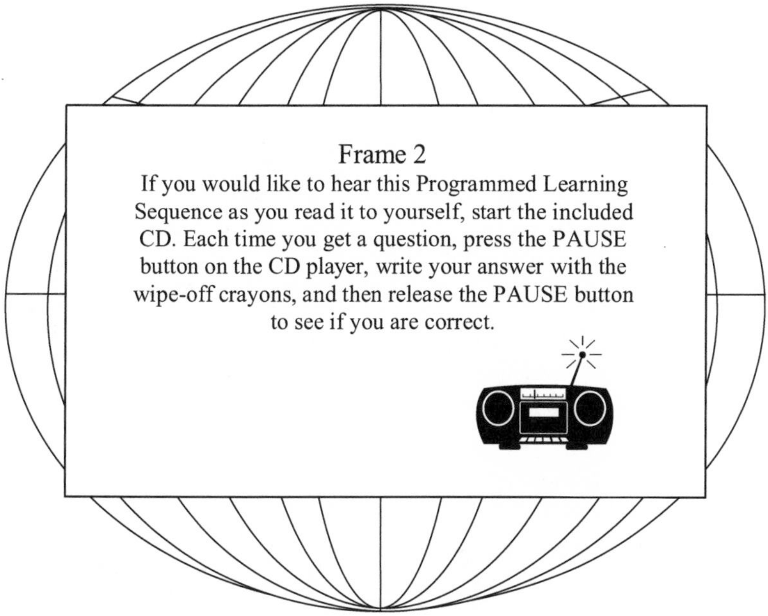

Frame 2
If you would like to hear this Programmed Learning Sequence as you read it to yourself, start the included CD. Each time you get a question, press the PAUSE button on the CD player, write your answer with the wipe-off crayons, and then release the PAUSE button to see if you are correct.

Back of Frame 2
Ready? Hope so!

Figure 9.1. (*continued*)

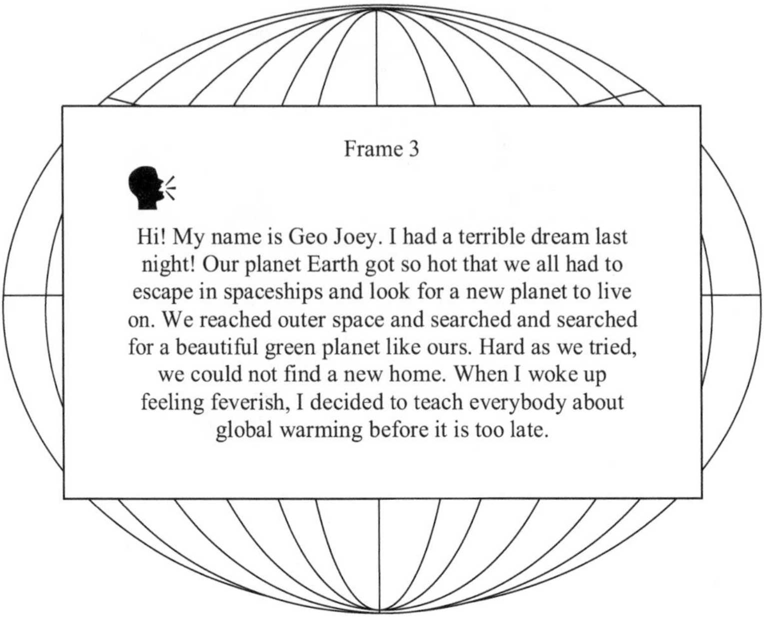

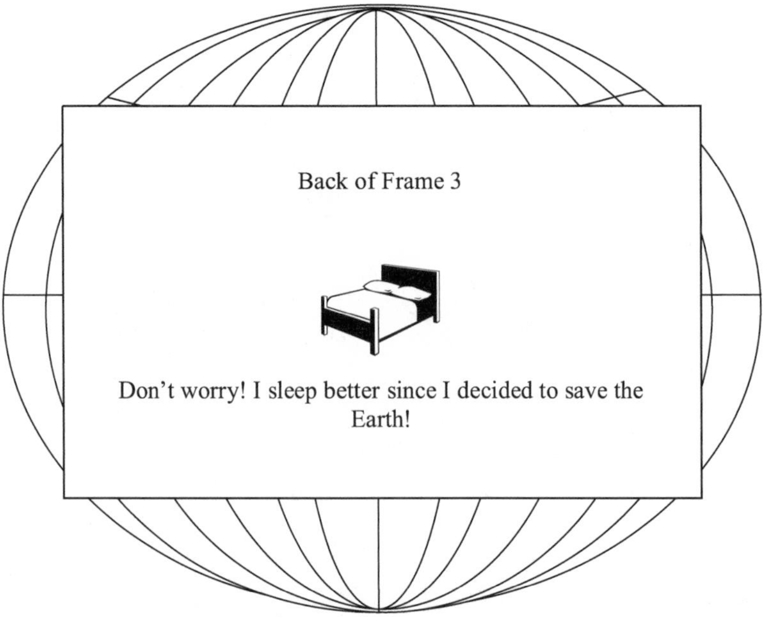

Figure 9.1. (*continued*)

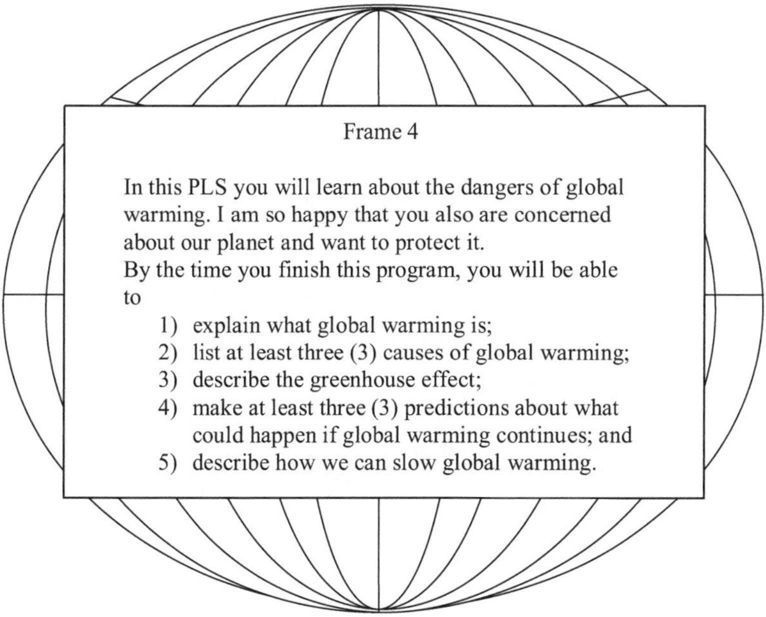

Frame 4
In this PLS you will learn about the dangers of global warming. I am so happy that you also are concerned about our planet and want to protect it.
By the time you finish this program, you will be able to
1) explain what global warming is;
2) list at least three (3) causes of global warming;
3) describe the greenhouse effect;
4) make at least three (3) predictions about what could happen if global warming continues; and
5) describe how we can slow global warming.

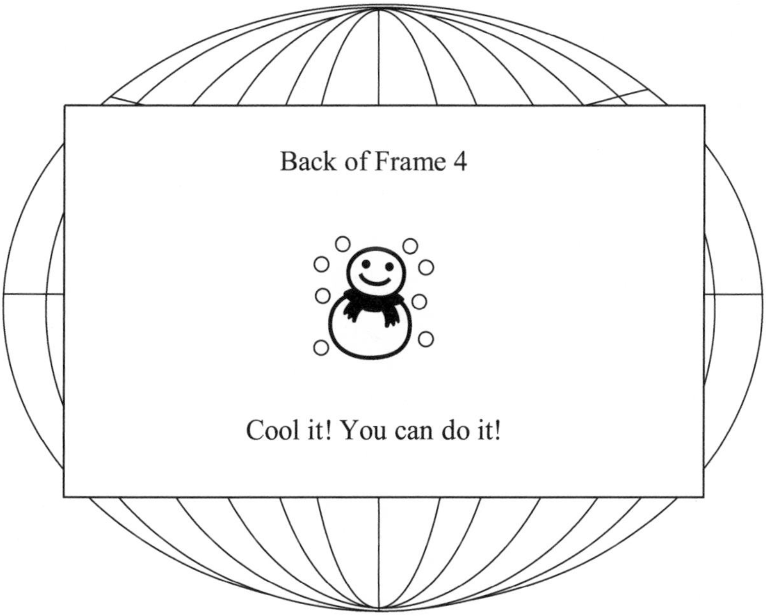

Back of Frame 4
Cool it! You can do it!

Figure 9.1. (*continued*)

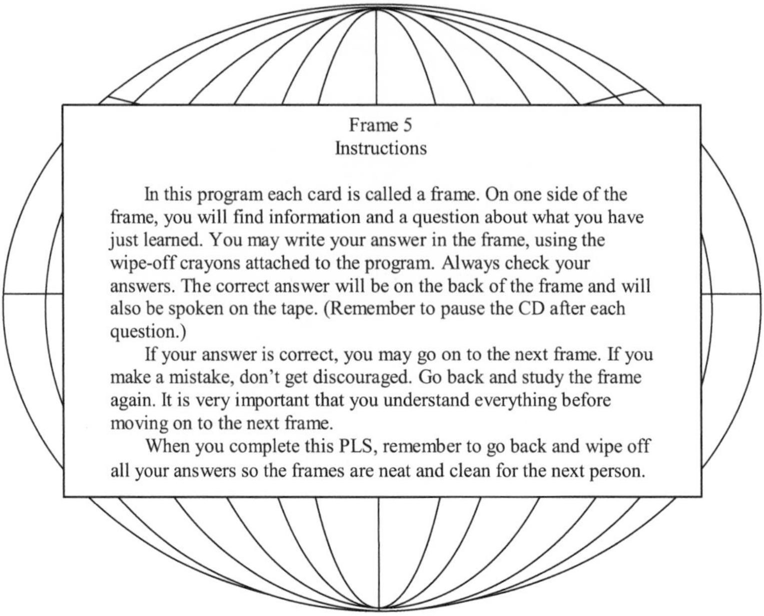

Frame 5
Instructions

In this program each card is called a frame. On one side of the frame, you will find information and a question about what you have just learned. You may write your answer in the frame, using the wipe-off crayons attached to the program. Always check your answers. The correct answer will be on the back of the frame and will also be spoken on the tape. (Remember to pause the CD after each question.)

If your answer is correct, you may go on to the next frame. If you make a mistake, don't get discouraged. Go back and study the frame again. It is very important that you understand everything before moving on to the next frame.

When you complete this PLS, remember to go back and wipe off all your answers so the frames are neat and clean for the next person.

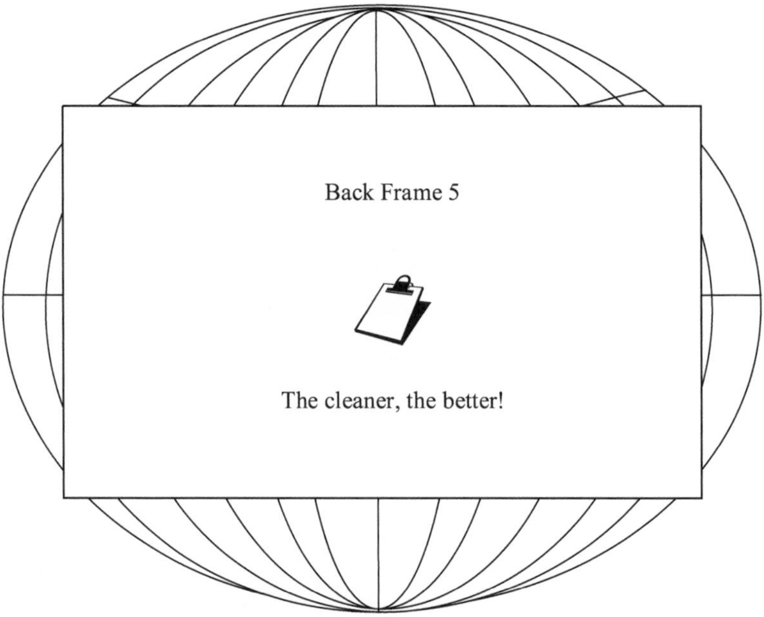

Back Frame 5

The cleaner, the better!

Figure 9.1. (*continued*)

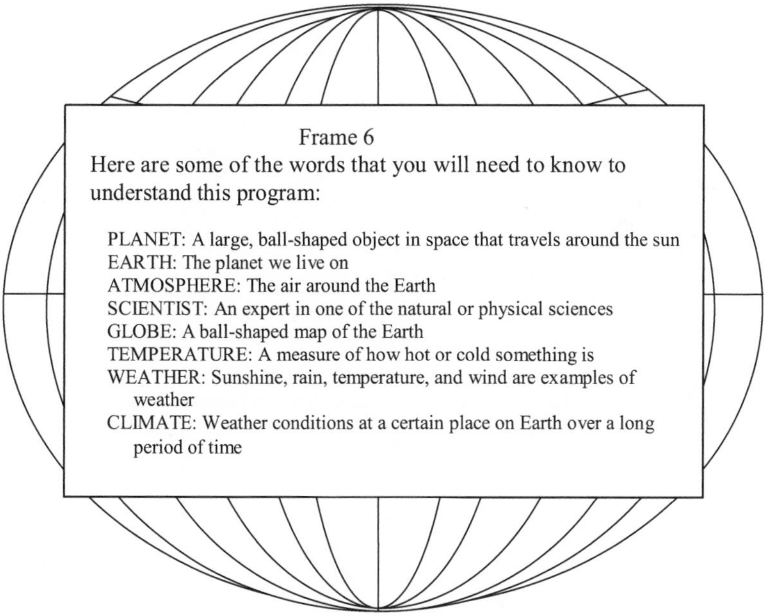
Frame 6
Here are some of the words that you will need to know to understand this program:
PLANET: A large, ball-shaped object in space that travels around the sun
EARTH: The planet we live on
ATMOSPHERE: The air around the Earth
SCIENTIST: An expert in one of the natural or physical sciences
GLOBE: A ball-shaped map of the Earth
TEMPERATURE: A measure of how hot or cold something is
WEATHER: Sunshine, rain, temperature, and wind are examples of weather
CLIMATE: Weather conditions at a certain place on Earth over a long period of time

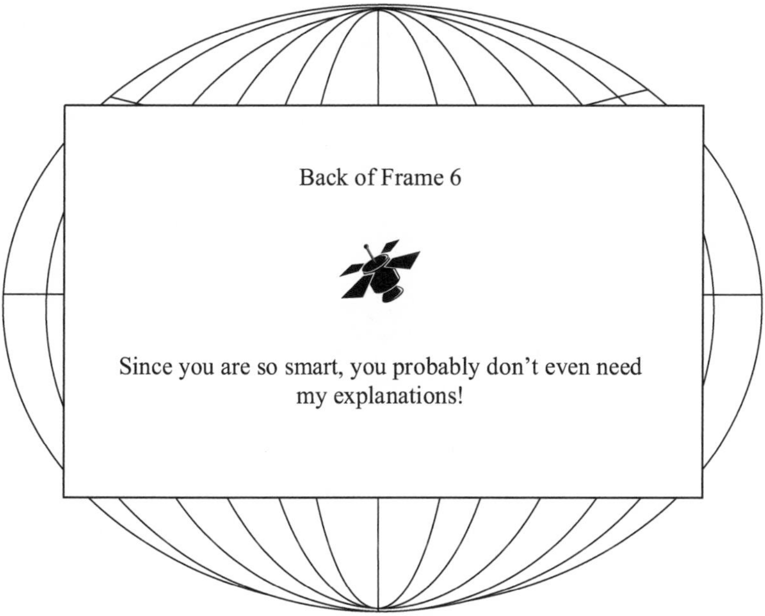
Back of Frame 6
Since you are so smart, you probably don't even need my explanations!

Figure 9.1. **(*continued*)**

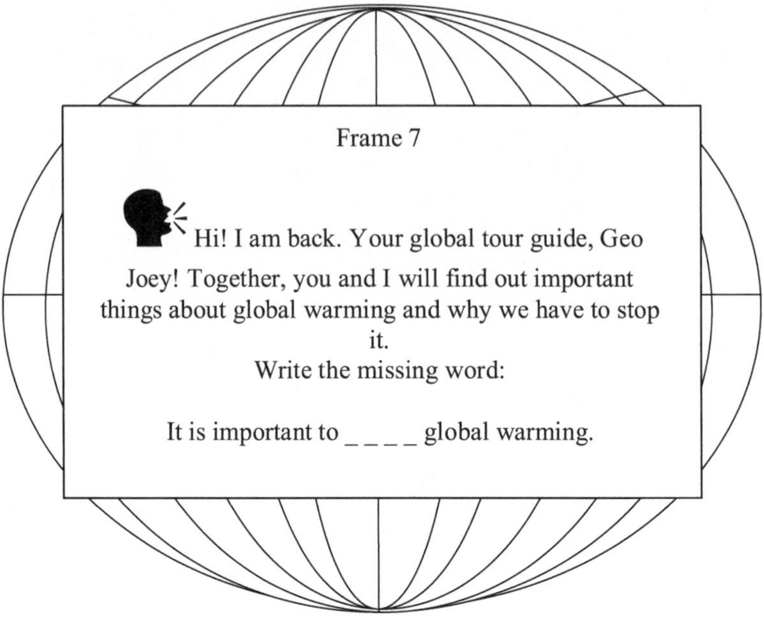

Frame 7
Hi! I am back. Your global tour guide, Geo Joey! Together, you and I will find out important things about global warming and why we have to stop it.
Write the missing word:
It is important to _ _ _ _ global warming.

Back of Frame 7
It is important to S T O P global warming.
We have to slow global warming down.

Figure 9.1. (*continued*)

Frame 8

Reach into the box and find a soft, blue and green ball. (I'll wait for you, just press pause on the CD player.) The ball you are holding in your hand is a globe. Our planet Earth looks somewhat like this from space. The green areas show land and the blue areas show oceans on the globe.

A ball-shaped map is called a ___________________.

Back of Frame 8

A ball-shaped map is called a ___globe___.

I hope you are having **a *ball*** with this PLS!

Figure 9.1. (*continued*)

Frame 9

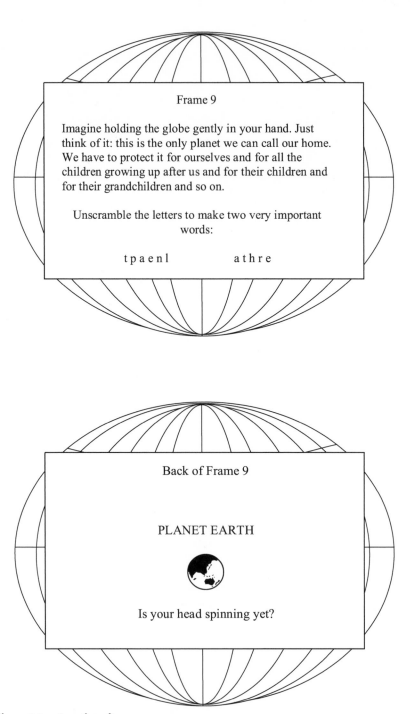

Imagine holding the globe gently in your hand. Just think of it: this is the only planet we can call our home. We have to protect it for ourselves and for all the children growing up after us and for their children and for their grandchildren and so on.

Unscramble the letters to make two very important words:

t p a e n l   a t h r e

Back of Frame 9

PLANET EARTH

Is your head spinning yet?

Figure 9.1. (***continued***)

Frame 10

Global warming is a worldwide problem. It affects everybody on earth, that's why it is called global. Most scientists agree that our planet seems to be heating up. Weather conditions are changing around the world. If the temperature on the Earth rises by just a few degrees in the next 50 years, it will dramatically change the climate around the world. Geo Joey will tell you why it is so dangerous after you answer this question:

Most scientists agree that the Earth is ________________.

(1) not changing (2) cooling off (3) heating up

Back of Frame 10

Most scientists agree that the Earth is _heating up_.

It's getting a little hot in here, too!

Now that you understand the basic concepts, it is time for a review. The next frame is an Electroboard. Take out the continuity-tester and see how many words on the left you can match with the explanations on the right.

Figure 9.1. (***continued***)

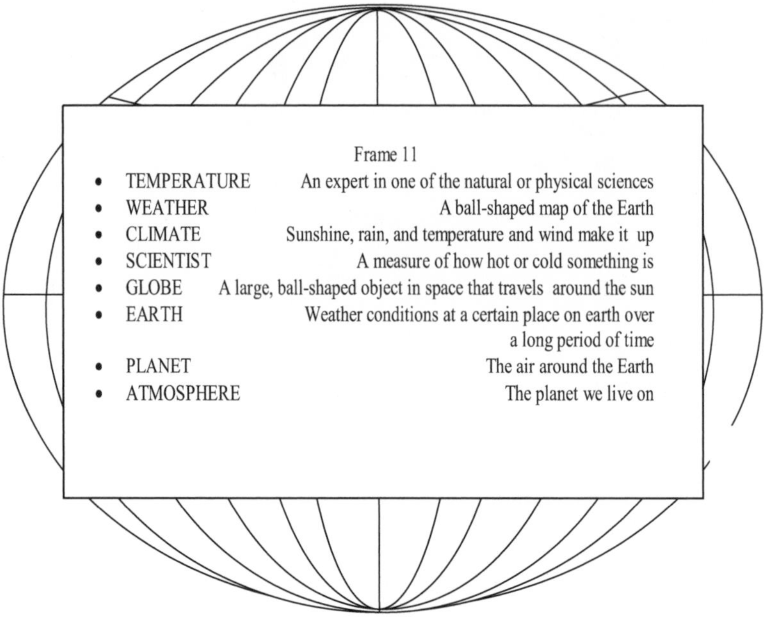
Frame 11
• TEMPERATURE
• WEATHER
• CLIMATE
• SCIENTIST
• GLOBE
• EARTH
• PLANET
• ATMOSPHERE
An expert in one of the natural or physical sciences
A ball-shaped map of the Earth
Sunshine, rain, and temperature and wind make it up
A measure of how hot or cold something is
A large, ball-shaped object in space that travels around the sun
Weather conditions at a certain place on earth over a long period of time
The air around the Earth
The planet we live on

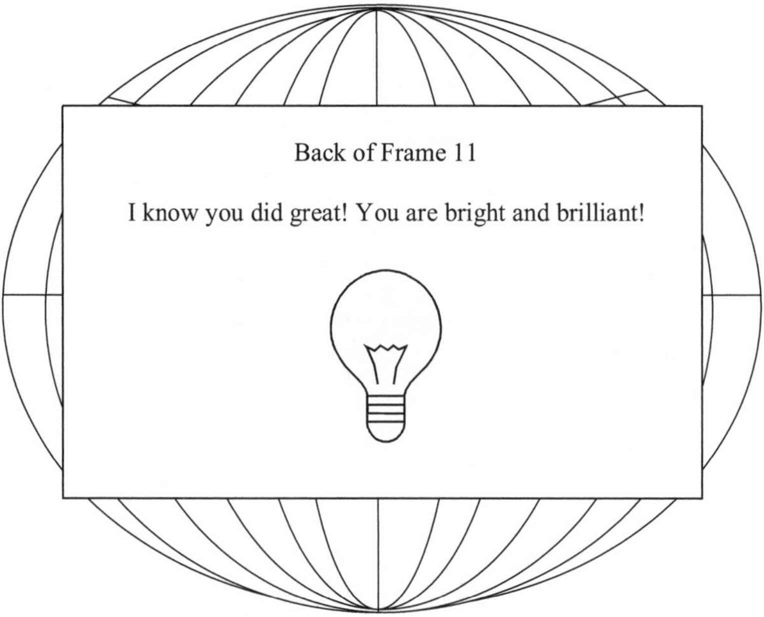
Back of Frame 11
I know you did great! You are bright and brilliant!

Figure 9.1. (*continued*)

Frame 12

On his spin around the world, Geo Joey saw people pollute the air everywhere he went. The world is warming up mainly because people burn coal, oil, and gas to make power, to run cars, and to heat homes and offices. The smoke from burning coal, oil, and gas pollutes the air, so more and more heat gets trapped in the Earth's atmosphere.

List three energy sources people burn:

Back of Frame 12

The three energy sources people burn are:
coal, oil, and gas.

The race is on!
Which race? The race to save the Earth, of course!

Figure 9.1. (*continued*)

Frame 13

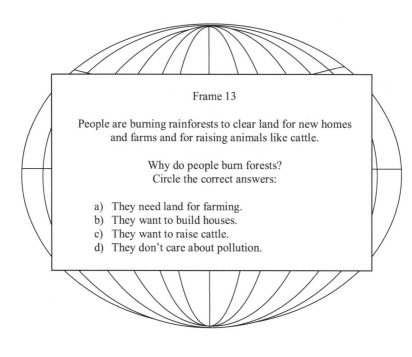

People are burning rainforests to clear land for new homes and farms and for raising animals like cattle.

Why do people burn forests?
Circle the correct answers:

a) They need land for farming.
b) They want to build houses.
c) They want to raise cattle.
d) They don't care about pollution.

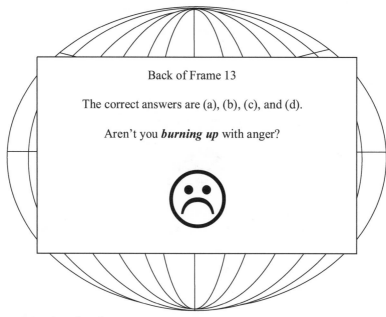

Back of Frame 13

The correct answers are (a), (b), (c), and (d).

Aren't you ***burning up*** with anger?

Figure 9.1. ***(continued)***

Frame 14

Trees are extremely important in our lives. As trees grow, they use carbon dioxide, which is the air that you breathe out. At the same time, trees make oxygen, a gas all animals and people need to survive.
Trees are crucial for our survival. They use what we breathe out in order to produce oxygen, which we need to breathe in.

On his trip around the world, Geo Joey was devastated to see entire forests destroyed. No wonder he had a nightmare! When people cut down the trees in a forest it is called deforestation. Trees are very important to us because they produce oxygen. Cutting down trees is really dangerous. There is less oxygen in the air and more carbon dioxide, also called CO_2.

CO_2 is a symbol for which words?

Back of Frame 14

Carbon dioxide.

You must be a genius to spell that right. But if you made a mistake, don't worry, the first time I wrote it, I did too.

Figure 9.1. ***(continued)***

Frame 15

Carbon dioxide (CO_2), other gasses in the air, and pollution are responsible for the greenhouse effect. Greenhouses, which are built to grow vegetables and exotic plants year round in colder climates, are wonderful inventions. The greenhouse effect is not great! Making the entire Earth hotter than natural is dangerous.

Draw a diagram and label it using the following terms:
(1) Sun (2) Earth (3) Atmosphere

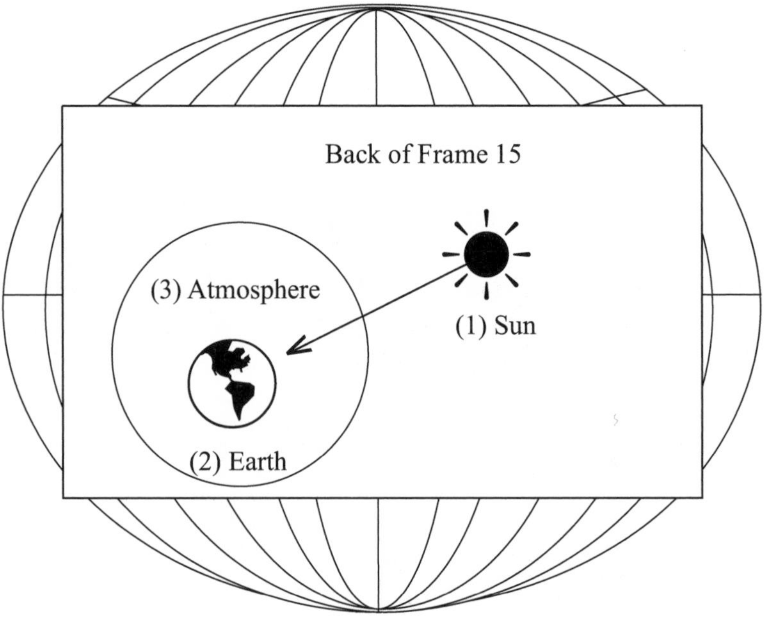

Figure 9.1. ***(continued)***

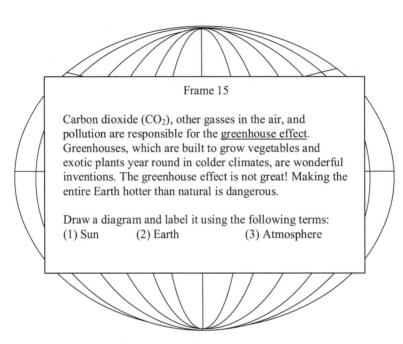

Frame 16

The greenhouse effect traps heat in our atmosphere much like a greenhouse traps heat. These are the steps:

1. Sunlight passes through the atmosphere
2. The Earth heats up
3. Heat tries to leave Earth but is trapped in the atmosphere

Fill in the missing words in the following explanation of the greenhouse effect:

As ____________________ passes through the atmosphere, the ____________________ heats up. The ____________________ tries to escape but is trapped by the ______________________________.

Back of Frame 16

As sunlight passes through the atmosphere, the Earth heats up. The heat tries to escape but is trapped by the atmosphere.

Time is running out to make a difference!

Figure 9.1. ***(continued)***

Frame 17

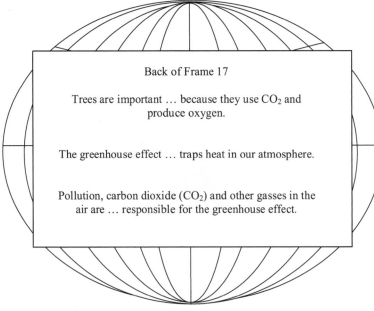

Let's review what we have learned about the greenhouse effect and climate changes so far.
Take out the Task Cards from the envelope and match them:

Trees are important … >
The greenhouse effect … >
Pollution, carbon dioxide (CO_2), and other gasses in the air are … >

< … responsible for the greenhouse effect.
< … because they use CO_2 and produce oxygen.
< … traps heat in our atmosphere.

Back of Frame 17

Trees are important … because they use CO_2 and produce oxygen.

The greenhouse effect … traps heat in our atmosphere.

Pollution, carbon dioxide (CO_2) and other gasses in the air are … responsible for the greenhouse effect.

Figure 9.1. ***(continued)***

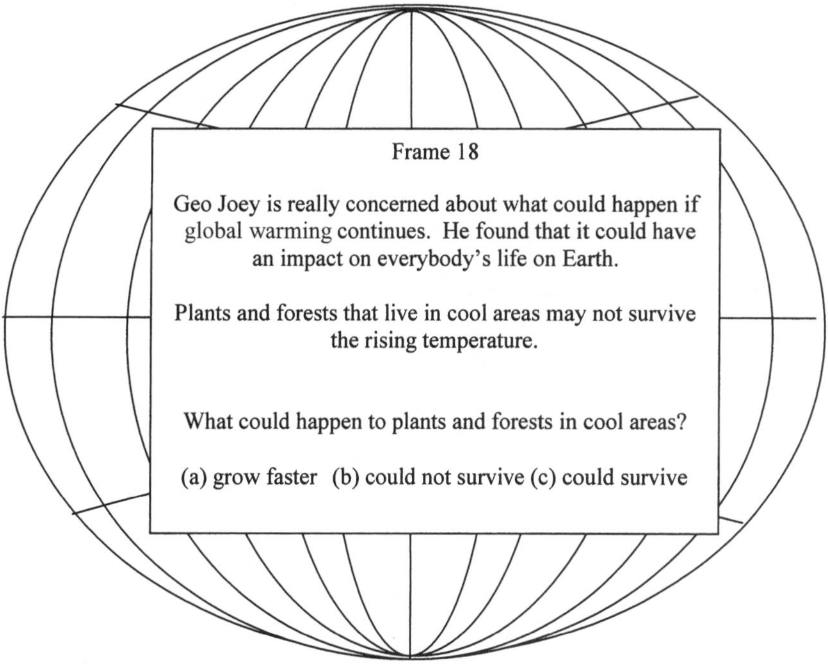
Frame 18
Geo Joey is really concerned about what could happen if global warming continues. He found that it could have an impact on everybody's life on Earth.
Plants and forests that live in cool areas may not survive the rising temperature.
What could happen to plants and forests in cool areas?
(a) grow faster (b) could not survive (c) could survive

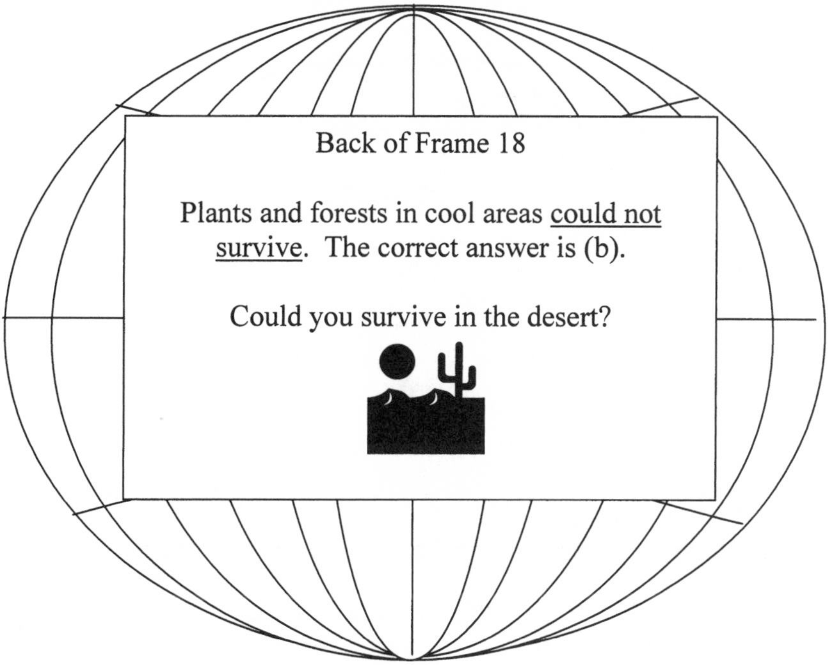
Back of Frame 18
Plants and forests in cool areas could not survive. The correct answer is (b).
Could you survive in the desert?

Figure 9.1. (***continued***)

Frame 19

Some scientists predict that the polar ice caps will melt. This could cause more rain in the polar areas. It could also raise the sea level around the world. Some cities right on the coast could be flooded.

What could be in danger of flooding because of the melting ice caps?

(a) rivers (b) rain forests (c) cities on the coast

Back of Frame 19

The correct answer is (c).

Cities on the coast could be in danger of flooding because of the melting ice caps.

That would not be a day on the beach!

Figure 9.1. ***(continued)***

Frame 20

Geo Joey is ready to put you on the right track. You can do a lot to slow down global warming. You won't believe your eyes and ears!

Cars pollute the air by adding dangerous gases to the air. Pollution also causes the greenhouse effect. So use your bike or walk instead of driving your car so much.

Why would walking or riding a bike help protect the Earth?

Back of Frame 20

Because you don't pollute the air.

You'll also be in great shape. So come on, right after you complete this PLS, get those walking shoes or your bike out!

Figure 9.1. ***(continued)***

Frame 21

Turn off lights and your TV when you don't need them. Use your air conditioner only when somebody is at home. If you are wondering about the logical connection here, here is an explanation for you.

If you use less electricity, power plants will produce less power, so they won't burn so much gas or oil.

List at least three electrical appliances you can turn off when you don't need them in order to save energy:

Back of Frame 21

Lights, televisions, and air conditioners are only three appliances I mentioned. If you wrote more than three, you can make up a word search puzzle using all the electrical appliances you listed. Give your teacher your word search after you have completed the PLS, and you can challenge the whole class with it!

Figure 9.1. ***(continued)***

Frame 22

Save energy. Turn down the heat in your house or apartment if you don't need it. Wear a sweater instead of a T-shirt in winter and you'll save a lot of energy.

One way of saving energy is by turning down the ________ in your home.

Back of Frame 22

One way of saving energy is by turning down the heat in your home.

Of course if you have a strong preference for warm temperature, I would not want you to freeze in your own home.

Figure 9.1. ***(continued)***

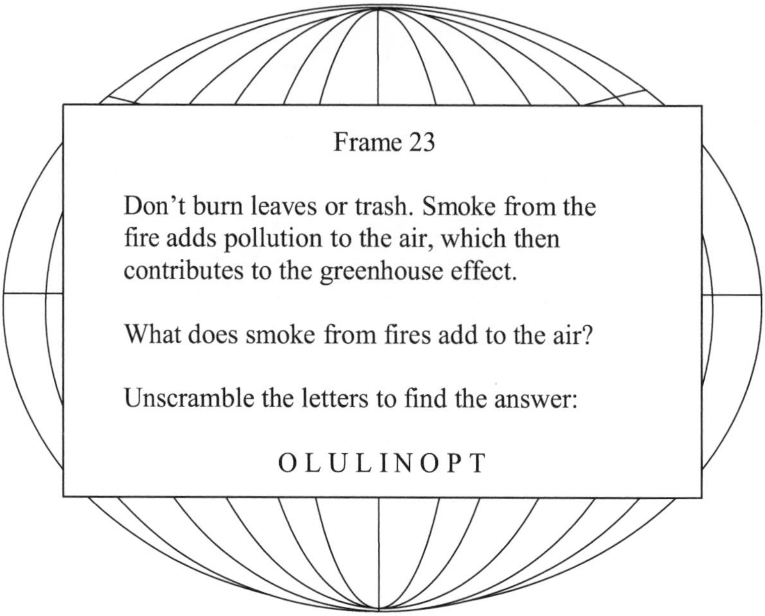

Frame 23
Don't burn leaves or trash. Smoke from the fire adds pollution to the air, which then contributes to the greenhouse effect.
What does smoke from fires add to the air?
Unscramble the letters to find the answer:
O L U L I N O P T

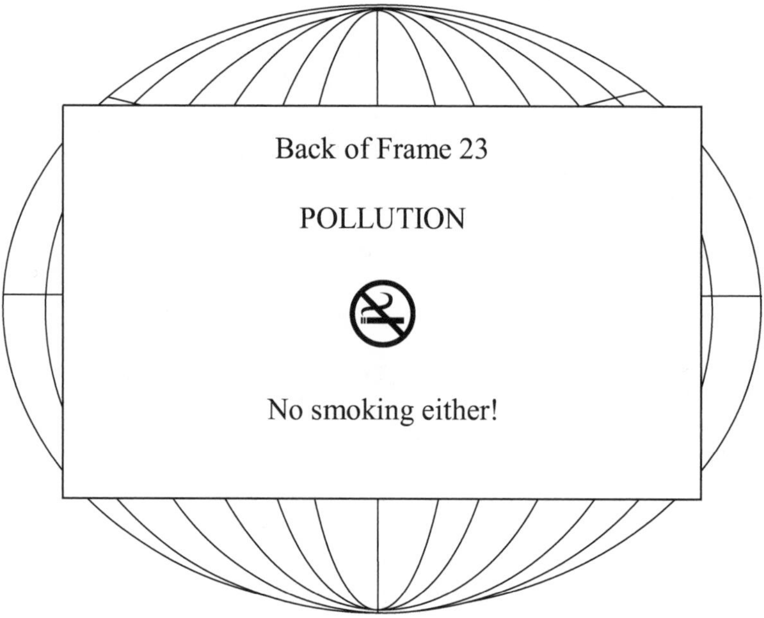

Figure 9.1. (*continued*)

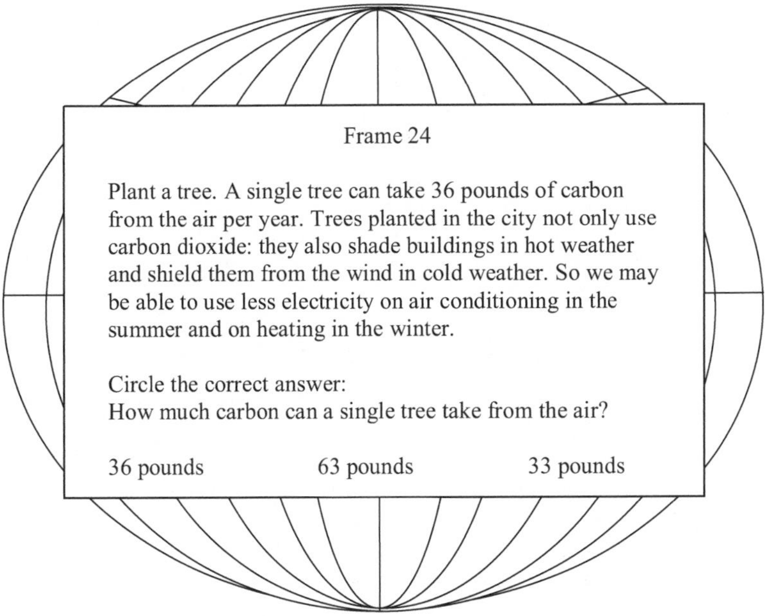
Frame 24
Plant a tree. A single tree can take 36 pounds of carbon from the air per year. Trees planted in the city not only use carbon dioxide: they also shade buildings in hot weather and shield them from the wind in cold weather. So we may be able to use less electricity on air conditioning in the summer and on heating in the winter.
Circle the correct answer:
How much carbon can a single tree take from the air?
36 pounds
63 pounds
33 pounds

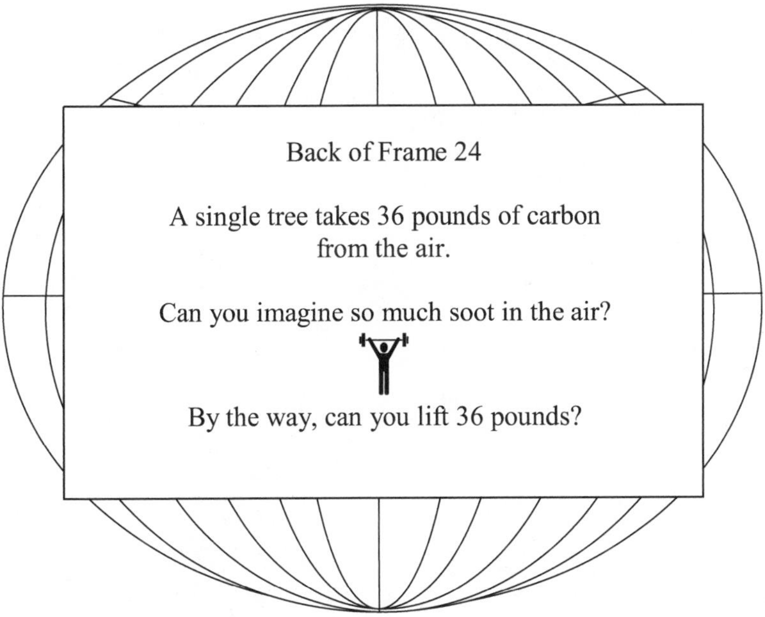
Back of Frame 24
A single tree takes 36 pounds of carbon from the air.
Can you imagine so much soot in the air?
By the way, can you lift 36 pounds?

Figure 9.1. ***(continued)***

Frame 25

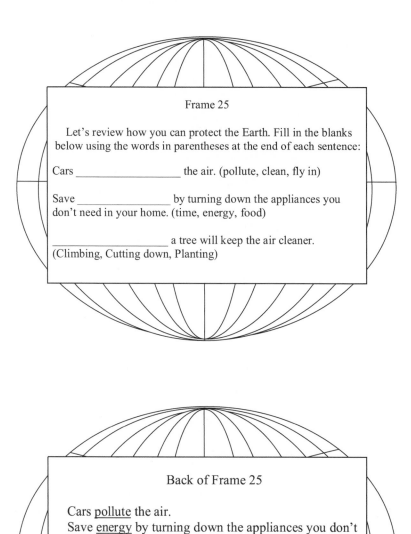

Let's review how you can protect the Earth. Fill in the blanks below using the words in parentheses at the end of each sentence:

Cars ___________________ the air. (pollute, clean, fly in)

Save ________________ by turning down the appliances you don't need in your home. (time, energy, food)

___________________ a tree will keep the air cleaner. (Climbing, Cutting down, Planting)

Back of Frame 25

Cars pollute the air.
Save energy by turning down the appliances you don't need in your home.
Planting a tree will keep the air cleaner.

So turn the light off!
(Have you heard that from anyone before?)

Figure 9.1. ***(continued)***

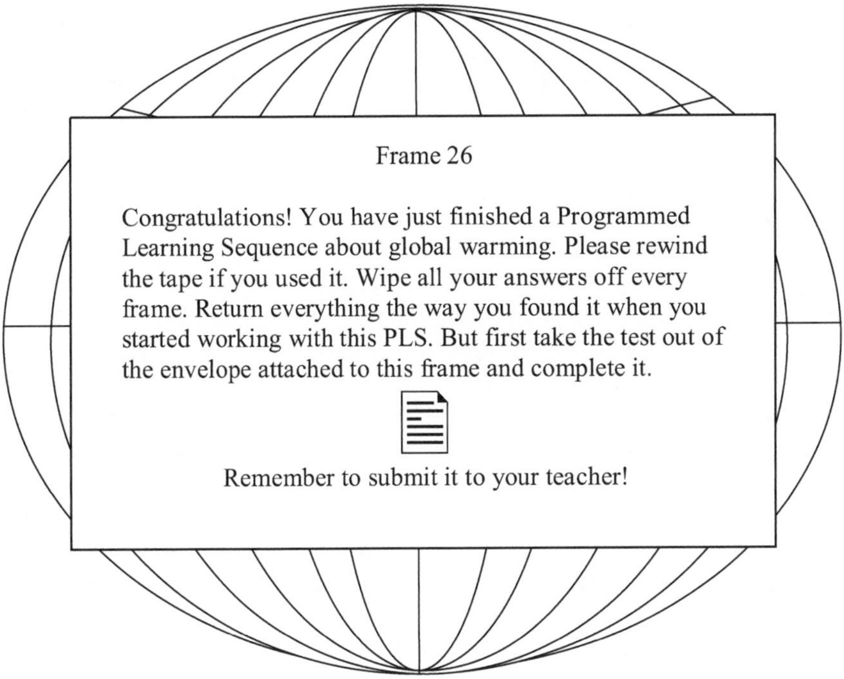

Figure 9.1. ***(continued)***

Many other full PLSs are available for comparison in Dunn and Dunn (1992, 1993, 1999); Carbo et al. (1986); Dunn and Blake (2008); and at www.learningstyles.net listed under Resources. This website has many "matched" PLSs and CAPs available for interested educators and parents.

WAYS TO INTEGRATE TECHNOLOGY INTO A PLS

A PLS is very effective as an interactive, colorful, illustrated booklet because students can become involved with the storyline, read the text and/or listen to it on the computer soundtrack or audio recording, and manipulate its tactual reinforcements either independently or in a pair. However, both the interactive nature of this learning tool and its audio-visual input can be replicated with advanced technology. An illustrated PowerPoint slide presentation with embedded hyperlinks can take the students through the content as an alternate printed resource. The sound-recording feature of the PowerPoint also allows for auditory input. Teachers can record themselves as they read the text aloud on each frame. An alternative to the inserted sound feature of PowerPoint is recording the voiceover using an MP3 player.

SmartBoard technology permits small groups or an entire class to work on a Programmed Learning Sequence presented as a PowerPoint. Students write their answers on the SmartBoard with electronic pens. Students' answers can be saved for later review by them or as informal assessment data by the teacher.

ASSESSING STUDENT PERFORMANCE

A PLS is designed to teach difficult content incrementally and immediately assess (and reinforce) the information presented on each frame. Every frame presents a manageable, well-defined piece of information and ends with a question, a sentence starter, or a short task. The back of each frame gives immediate feedback by stating the correct answer and a bit of teasing or joking. As such, a PLS itself assesses students' achievement because it gives them opportunities to manage their own learning with its questions and answers, the built-in manipulatives, and the final test directly related to its objectives. Students may reread the frames if they missed the correct answers. The PLS, similar to the Contract Activity Package presented in chapter 8, ends with the same formal unit test. The purpose of this tool is to assess *all* the learning that took place while the students worked with the PLS. Therefore, the PLS offers both formative and summative assessment on the content.

GRAPHIC GUIDE TO THE IMPLEMENTATION OF PROGRAMMED LEARNING SEQUENCES

If you want to know where in the process PLSs go, they tend to be implemented in the sequence presented in textbox 9.1—although you certainly could try using a PLS with visual and tactual students, who may need structure, without using other learning-style strategies.

REFLECTION POINTS

1. Start small and create a mini PLS for one learning objective for an upcoming unit you will be teaching. Create six to eight frames only and end your mini PLS with a tactual review activity such as an Electroboard, a set of Task Cards, or a Pic-A-Hole. Try your resource with a small group of

Textbox 9.1. Where Do PLSs Fit into the Learning-Styles Implementation Process?

STAGE 1

Learning-Styles Assessment
(See www.learningstyles.net for LS assessment tools)

- Share information with students, parents, all teachers.
- Help students use LS profiles and study guides to become self-directed learners.
- Raise awareness about time-of-day energy levels.
- Make adaptations for global vs. analytic teaching.

STAGE 2

Initial Implementation Steps

- Environmental accommodations (Room redesign)
- Methodologies and resources to respond to perceptual preferences
- Small-group instructional techniques

STAGE 3

Advanced Implementation Steps

- Contract Activity Packages
- *Programmed Learning Sequences*

students for whom the PLS is likely to work and gather information from them about its effectiveness and appeal.

2. Once you have seen how successful your students are with your mini PLS, share your experiences with colleagues who have not tried it. Invite two or three of them to develop one or two PLSs with you collaboratively. Try both the print versions and the electronic versions.

Chapter Ten

Teaching Unmotivated At-Risk Students with Multisensory Instructional Packages

Whenever this teaching team gets together for its bimonthly meeting to analyze their student challenges and help each other explore possible interventions, Marcus is invariably the first student they discuss. As the school year progresses, he has more and more trouble keeping up with required readings. He finds his seventh-grade homework "boring, hard, and too much to tackle." During independent work in class, his mind often wanders and he submits fewer completed assignments each week. Marcus and his teachers have had several conferences with his parents to discuss this ongoing problem.

The teachers on this team have tried several strategies with only limited success. For example, Marcus was assigned a buddy to work with on a couple of units; the two apparently had little in common and did not get along well. Marcus also was invited to review materials with a peer tutor from the eighth grade. When that didn't prove successful, the team gave him a Contract Activity Package to try. That resource wasn't anything the boy could handle on his own. No one on the team disliked Marcus; indeed, they sympathized with him. They just didn't know how to get him interested in learning.

At today's team meeting, Marcus's homeroom teacher, Mrs. Levine, enthusiastically reports that a new approach she tried two weeks ago seems to be working. To introduce this method, she places a large, colorful box in front of her colleagues. She describes how she presented the last two social studies units on the evolution of European society during the Middle Ages and the political, economic, and cultural transformations during the Renaissance. Mrs. Levine had designed a Multisensory Instructional Package (MIP) for Marcus and several other at-risk students about whom she was concerned. Mrs. Levine's colleagues respond with interest and enthusiasm as they examine the MIP, just as Marcus had. Almost like the adolescents they were teaching, the team of teachers examine the items in the colorful box and work through the multisensory materials diligently. "This is really well done!" they exclaim.

CHARACTERISTICS OF STUDENTS FOR WHOM MULTISENSORY INSTRUCTIONAL PACKAGES WORK

How does a Multisensory Instructional Package work for at-risk students? It is designed to respond to individuals' learning-style preferences and, as its name indicates, it also provides for their varied perceptual strengths. Youngsters with auditory, visual, tactual, or kinesthetic preferences each find suggestions for mastering the content in a way that appeals to and motivates them. An MIP, a Contract Activity Package, and a Programmed Learning Sequence all address the same objectives. In an MIP, several supporting tactual and kinesthetic resources help learners understand and remember the content in different ways.

The MIP is designed with numerous built-in choices so that even the most nonconforming students can find an entry point to the content. Once unmotivated learners get hooked on the topic through the first activity they use to respond to how they learn most easily, additional resources are available for them to further explore it. An MIP offers many choices and alternate routes to studying the material.

DESCRIPTION OF MULTISENSORY INSTRUCTIONAL PACKAGES

If you are interested in designing an MIP, follow these suggestions: Use a box as small as a shoe box or as big as one in which you might store blankets or a wedding dress. Fill the box with a set of carefully designed learning-style responsive materials that are all teacher or student created. As students lift and turn back the lid of the MIP, they should find a brief printed listing of the unit's objectives and the resources through which to master them, inside the box. Auditory students—or those who might have difficulty reading the contents—can be told to listen to the identical instructions on an accompanying recording.

Components of a Multisensory Instructional Package

Because an MIP usually is designed to teach a unit of study to students with different traits, the box that contains the materials typically includes the following resources:

1. one Contract Activity Package (CAP);
2. one Programmed Learning Sequence (PLS);
3. one recording that reads the text of the PLS and its directions;
4. several tactual resources;
5. one Floor Game;
6. one unit test; and
7. one set of directions (on tape or CD for young students or those who do not read well).

A SAMPLE MULTISENSORY INSTRUCTIONAL PACKAGE DESIGNED FOR AT-RISK STUDENTS

Below is a sample introduction sheet from an MIP designed for at-risk students on the topic of global warming. It was developed to illustrate the content and format of an MIP. In chapters 8 and 9, you saw that the Contract Activity Package and Programmed Learning Sequence address identical objectives. The MIP on global warming has both of those resources included in addition to numerous other instructional activities such as a set of Task Cards that teach about the greenhouse effect, an Electroboard about the causes of global warming, a Pic-A-Hole that reviews the impact of global warming, and a Save the Earth Floor Game.

Global Warming: It's Not Cool!

Hi! You are about to start using a Multisensory Instructional Package about global warming. I am pleased you are interested in protecting the Earth and learning about the dangers it is facing. I hope it will be both educational and enjoyable for you. Read through this introduction and listen to the entire recording before you start working.

By the time you finish this package you will be able to:

1. explain what global warming is;
2. list at least three (3) causes of global warming;
3. describe the "greenhouse" effect;
4. make at least three (3) predictions about what could happen if global warming continues; and
5. describe how we can slow down global warming.

In this MIP you will find:

1. a Contract Activity Package (also called a CAP);
2. a Programmed Learning Sequence (also called a PLS);

3. a recording that accompanies the PLS;
4. an Electroboard;
5. a Flip Chute;
6. Multipart Task Cards (a puzzle);
7. a Floor Game;
8. an assessment to show how much you learned; and
9. a small globe.

Begin learning about this topic by using the resource that best matches your own learning style. Afterward you may use all the other activities that you find interesting.

- If you are tactual, start with the golden Flip Chute, the tree-shaped Electroboard, or the Multipart Task Cards in the red pocket in any order you like.
- If you are kinesthetic, start with the Floor Game.
- If you are visual and like structure, start with the Programmed Learning Sequence. That is the storybook shaped like a world map. You also will find some tactual resources built onto the frames of the PLS.
- If you are auditory, remember to listen to the recording that accompanies the PLS.
- If you are self-motivated and enjoy having choices, start with the Contract Activity Package.

After you have finished an activity, please carefully put it back inside this MIP box. You can take a short break any time you need. After you have finished the entire package, you can check to see how much you have learned by taking the assessment you find at the end of the CAP or the PLS. Well, let's get rolling!

WHAT DOES AN MIP LOOK LIKE?

The entire MIP is depicted in the photograph below. The picture shows the attractive yet affordable teacher-created design of the MIP. All instructional resources fit into one clear plastic box (always available at Staples or in many hardware or department stores). Each component is aligned with the same objectives identified in the CAP and PLS. Each tactual and kinesthetic resource may be used independently, in pairs, or in small groups, so that, when taken apart, each MIP component serves as a single instructional tool for several students required to master the identical objectives.

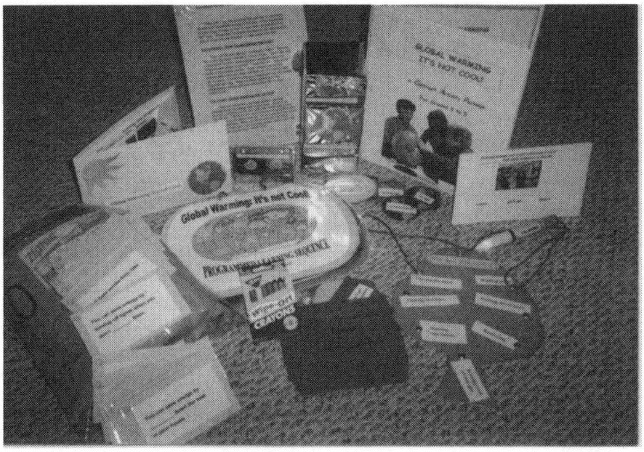

Global Warming MIP.

ASSESSING STUDENT PERFORMANCE

Assessment through MIPs is twofold. Since everything is self-corrective, students are encouraged to develop independence and self-reliance as they progress through it. They learn to assume responsibility for their own achievement and have opportunities to frequently assess themselves though the self-corrective tactual resources and Floor or Wall Game and the PLS answers on the back of each frame. The unit test that is presented at the end of the Contract Activity Package and the Programmed Learning Sequence offers the same formative assessment.

GRAPHIC GUIDE TO THE IMPLEMENTATION OF MULTISENSORY INSTRUCTIONAL PACKAGES

The Multisensory Instructional Package is considered the final and most ambitious step when implementing a learning-styles-based instructional program. Most other materials, resources, and strategies are incorporated into the MIP. Each of the strategies presented earlier can be used independently of each other. However, putting them together and guiding at-risk youngsters to use the resources most likely to facilitate mastery is an intriguing approach because it allows many choices of resources with which they can achieve in a legitimate manner the same goals as their classmates. We recommend that you experiment with the MIP and allow your students to enjoy the full benefits of this comprehensive learning-style-responsive tool.

Textbox 10.1. Where Do MIPs Fit into the Learning-Styles Implementation Process?

STAGE 1

Learning-Styles Assessment
(See www.learningstyles.net for LS assessment tools)

- Share information with students, parents, all teachers.
- Help students use LS profiles and study guides to become self-directed learners.
- Raise awareness about time-of-day energy levels.
- Make adaptations for global vs. analytic teaching.

STAGE 2

Initial Implementation Steps

- Environmental accommodations (Room redesign)
- Methodologies and resources to respond to perceptual preferences
- Small-group instructional techniques

STAGE 3

Advanced Implementation Steps

- Contract Activity Packages
- Programmed Learning Sequences
- *Multisensory Instructional Packages*

REFLECTION POINTS

1. Review the contents of the MIP and try to match each component with as many learning-style preferences as possible. Reflect on whether most of your at-risk students' needs are met by studying content this way.
2. Design an MIP on a unit of your choice. Try it with your students and then teach them how to work collaboratively to design and create as many components of the MIP as possible on their own. Administer the SDS Attitude Survey in Appendix A and see how much more they enjoy learning with an MIP than any other way.
3. Present your own and your students' MIPs to the larger school community at a Share Fair and invite feedback on these instructional resources.

Chapter Eleven

Experimenting with Learning-Style Instructional Strategies in Practitioner-Oriented Steps

Three, fourth-grade teachers attended the same district-sponsored staff development session on learning styles. The speaker had emphasized that many at-risk students physically cannot concentrate while seated in plastic, steel, or wooden chairs and desks. Those same children have trouble in bright lighting. He repeated that certain children only begin thinking in depth when on comfortable, informal seating or pillows placed in soft illumination. Such learners have to avoid physical stress before they can begin to focus on new and challenging curriculum content.

- The first teacher murmured, "If all it takes is some comfortable seating and lighting, I would give it a shot!"
- "But how do we get started? What should we do first?" the second one asked.
- "Whatever we do, let's do it in all three classrooms! We can help each other and then compare the results," said the third.

On the way back to school after lunch, the three agreed to see whether changing their classroom environments really improved their students' test scores. They didn't quite know how and with what to begin, and they certainly didn't have much money to spend. However, they compiled a list of things to try, citing what they might do first, second, and next. If you want to see whether a little classroom redesign improves students' test scores, consider which of the following steps you might try!

GETTING STARTED WITH LEARNING STYLES

Many learners of all ages cannot sit still for more than 10–15 minutes in conventional classroom seating. To focus well, they must be relaxed—as opposed to others who focus better when they are tense. Helping students relax does not have to be expensive; it does take a bit of thinking and creativity.

Beginning Steps for Designing a Responsive Environment

Try one or more of the following activities to begin redesigning your classroom. Working with another colleague or two reduces the number of steps each individual needs to take and makes the process move more quickly than when working alone. Choose those things for which you will assume responsibility. Do something today!

1. Ask for donations of pillows or cloth (with which to make new pillows or cover old ones) from manufacturers, local stores, or parents. You only may need enough pillows for about six or seven students. Not everyone wants a pillow on the chair or to sit on one on the floor.
2. Solicit a couple of summer garden-type chairs from parents for temporary classroom use.
3. Ask parents to contribute a couch or easy chair they may no longer want. Cover any faded fabric with an attractive shawl or throw.
4. Ask parents to contribute two or three high-pile, pretty bathroom throw rugs.
5. Take a neighborhood walk with the children and from local food stores collect clean, empty, durable cardboard boxes in which canned goods are delivered. These will become "bookcase dividers" to establish small personal "dens" and "library stations" (to reduce classroom hyperactivity, noises, and behavior problems.)
6. Solicit left-over cans of paint from each household or local paint stores.
7. Ask the school custodian to staple the cardboard boxes together to create low bookcases. These can house tactual and kinesthetic resources and serve as room dividers.
8. Have the students paint and decorate the emerging bookcases after they complete required assignments. Many parents and older siblings will help paint the bookcases if asked to do so.
9. Create two or three (or more) hip-high instructional areas as described in chapter 4. Use the bookcases perpendicular from classroom walls to provide children who prefer quiet and privacy their own "den," "work," "private," or "study" area.

However, pairs can occupy and share such an area and, if warranted, so can three or four—with the understanding that (a) no child's learning style may distract anyone, (b) all assignments must be completed, and (c) spoken words should not be decipherable by anyone occupying another area.

10. Place a line of colored tape and an attractive sign at the entrance to each instructional area.
11. Teach the children to remove their shoes and leave them outside each instructional area that houses a carpet, couch, easy chair, or rug.
12. Allow either only those who really need comfortable seating to use the informal instructional areas or alternate their use for different lessons or different students so that those who want to work that way may do so periodically.
13. Turn off one bank of lights away from windows so that the room has softly and brightly lit areas.
14. Purchase inexpensive light blue, green, or pink plastic covers for the bulbs in the darker section of the room to further subdue the lighting.
15. Arrange one softly illuminated section in each room. Place a couple of pretty, high-pile bathroom mats, pillows, or low plastic seats into each area.
16. Locate earplugs or earphones to provide additional quiet for those who are very sound sensitive. If the earphones work, allow students who need sound to hear concert or orchestral music without lyrics while they do assignments.
17. If asked to do so on official letterhead, airline companies might voluntarily and without cost contribute 50 plastic earplugs they distribute to passengers in flight.

Beginning Steps for Differentiating by Perceptual Strengths

1. Identify each student's perceptual strength with an age-appropriate instrument (see chapter 2).
2. Create a simple but attractive wall chart that denotes the strongly auditory, kinesthetic, tactual, and visual students in each class. Perhaps add a photo or drawing of each child's face to assist global students in internalizing their preferred instructional patterns. Colorfully graph the sequence of instructional resources that students with particular strengths should follow. Perhaps have students adapt figure 11.1 to their personal needs.
3. Urge at-risk students to begin concentrating with their strongest modality and to reinforce with their next strongest. If two are equally strong, allow individuals to choose the one they most like learning through.

MOST RESPONSIVE SEQUENCE OF INSTRUCTIONAL RESOURCES RELATED TO INDIVIDUAL STUDENTS' LEARNING-STYLE STRENGTHS

AUDITORY, VISUAL, MOTIVATED or NON-CONFORMING	MOSTLY TACTUAL	MOSTLY KINESTHETIC	VISUAL-TACTUAL, IN NEED OF STRUCTURE	WITHOUT PERCEPTUAL STRENGTHS
Contract Activity Package 	Tactual Resources 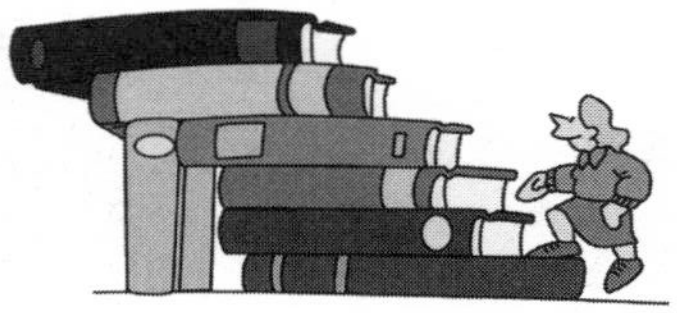 PLS with Tape or CD Available	Floor Game  PLS with Tape or CD Available	PLS with Tape or CD Tactual Resources Floor Game	Tactual / Kinesthetic Resources 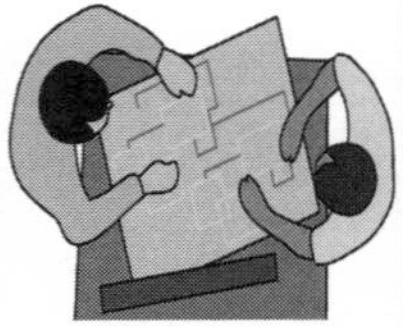 MIP / PLS with Tape or CD Available

⇒1 **All directions should be clear and illustrated.**
⇒2 **Students must begin the learning process according to this schema. Reinforcement through the secondary resource is likely to be extremely effective. However, if children strongly prefer an alternative reinforcement, permit that choice provided they demonstrate obvious improvement. Otherwise return to the schema.**

(Dunn & Guldahl, 2005)

Figure 11.1. Overview of Learning-Styles Implementation

4. Remind students to use their modality strengths when doing assignments at home.

A PLAN OF ACTION

Do you need to chart out your steps to learning-styles implementation? Why not try to use the action planner in figure 11.2 below? First, reflect on your own best practices and self-assess the degree to which you are already offering learning-styles-based instruction in your classroom. What are your areas of strength? With which of the elements have you successfully experimented? Perhaps you are aware of, and responsive to, your students' perceptual preferences. Perhaps you modify your instruction to better meet the needs of students who require global rather than analytical steps to learning. Go through the entire model, taking your time to reflect on each element and jot down all the things you've tried with which your students have been successful. Then be just as reflective and critical about the areas of learning style that you have not yet either partially or fully implemented. Once you have filled out the top part of the chart, move on to establishing short-term and long-term goals in the following three areas:

1. Implementation of the Dunn and Dunn model of learning styles
2. Instructional modifications to meet the needs of all students
3. Assessment modifications to meet the needs of all students

Beginning Steps for Administrators to Consider

1. Provide staff development for interested teachers and supervisors through the participants' learning styles. Use only certified learning-style trainers to provide this service. A list of certified trainers is available on www.learningstyles.net.
2. Have involved teachers each identify the school population with which to begin the learning-style process. Explain the concept and its practices to the students who will be involved and to their parents.
3. Use age-appropriate, reliable, and valid instruments to identify students' learning and teachers' teaching styles (www.learningstyles.net, click on Instruments.)
4. Assign students to classes based on their styles. For example, group the highly tactual students together and introduce new topics with Task Cards. You easily can teach children to make their own and require other tactuals for homework. Parents will help, as will upper-grade students and geriatric adults in nursing homes.

Self-Assessment of Offering Learning-Styles Based Instruction	
My strengths	**Areas needing attention**

	Short-term goals	Long-term goals
Implementation of the Dunn and Dunn model of learning styles		
Instructional modifications to meet the needs of all students		
Assessment modifications to meet the needs of all students		

Figure 11.2. Action Planning Template

Another possibility is to identify large clusters of kinesthetic youth (students who cannot sit at traditional desks for any length of time and who require movement while concentrating). For those, introduce new topics with Floor or Wall Games or huge Flip Chutes (made from refrigerator or washing machine boxes). Make large Magic Windows, Electroboards, or Pic-A-Holes.

5. Encourage teachers and supervisors to plan for and schedule those activities you might consider trying first, second, third, and so forth. Establish a flexible calendar of gradual implementation and the dates on which you want to observe them in classrooms (Braio et al., 1997; Klavas et al., 1994).
6. Make it known that lesson plans need to include notations concerning how students' different styles will be addressed or which youngsters will be working with which resources or methods.

7. Introduce one strategy at a time—perhaps one a week. The best strategies with which to begin are those that respond to individuals' (a) environmental, mobility, and tactual and/or kinesthetic strengths, (b) global-processing patterns, and/or (c) time-of-day energy levels.
8. Develop an illustrated chart to clearly describe class rules for learning with individuals' styles (Dunn, 1996). Share the chart with colleagues who seem interested in exploring learning-style strategies. Urge them to discuss the rules with their pupils so that no one misunderstands. Caution them to apply the rules firmly, but fairly.
9. Provide students with individual homework prescriptions based on their learning-style strengths as provided by individual profiles from LIVES, LS: CY!, and ELSA.
10. Experiment with small-group strategies for students who cannot learn/work independently (see chapter 7).
11. Experiment teaching with Floor Games for everyone (see chapter 6), but focus on the end-of-unit-tests for kinesthetic learners. Kinesthetic students should perform better with this strategy than with traditional teaching (Dunn & Dunn, 1992, 1993; Dunn et al., 1994). Indeed, many ADD and ADHD students appeared to have only a kinesthetic strength; many have no perceptual strength at all (Brand, 1999; Greb, 1999; Brand, Dunn, & Greb, 2002).
12. Experiment with a Programmed Learning Sequence (PLS) for everyone (See chapter 9), but compare the test scores of low-auditory students who need structure and are visual, motivated, and tactual. They will perform better with this strategy than with traditional teaching (Gremli, 1999; 2001–2002, 2007; Ming, 2004, 2007; Ming & Ansalone, 2006; Miller, Ostrow, Dunn, Beasley, Geisert, & Nelson, 2000–2001).
13. Experiment with a Contract Activity Package (see chapter 8) for everyone, but compare the test scores of nonconformists and independent learners. These students should perform better with this strategy than with traditional teaching (Gremli, 1999, 2001–2002, 2007; Lefkowitz, 2001, 2006, 2007).
14. Compare the achievement of students whose learning styles have been addressed during a lesson with the achievement of those same students when their styles have not been addressed.
15. Encourage students to express their feelings about learning style. Use the attitude assessment in appendix A to determine their reactions.
16. Share your and your students' successes. Keep at it. Encourage the children to develop their own strategies for teaching themselves with their learning-style strengths (Dunn & Dunn, 1993, Dunn et al., 1994).

17. For behavioral problems, use counseling strategies that respond to students' learning-style strengths (Griggs, 1991; Oberer, 2003). After one full year, assess students' achievement, attitudes, and behavior changes. Report the results to administrators, colleagues, parents, and students.

ASSESSING STUDENTS' ATTITUDES

Students' achieving better than they previously have is an important goal of instruction. However, having students enjoy learning may be equally as important. Therefore, we periodically should address their attitudes toward learning and toward a variety of instructional approaches—particularly if we are engaged in differentiating instruction. Differentiating, in and of itself, has little merit unless we accumulate evidence that our at-risk students are learning more and liking learning better than they did before we introduced the new strategies.

Comparing Attitudes toward Two Different Treatments

When we are interested in whether our at-risk students prefer learning more with one approach than with another, we use the Semantic Differential Survey (SDS) (Pizzo, 1981) to compare their attitudes toward two different strategies. The SDS compares attitudes toward learning with traditional teaching (TT) versus with a Multisensory Instructional Package (MIP) (Dunn & Dunn, 1993) or learning with a CAP versus with a PLS. The SDS includes 12 bipolar descriptive pairs that assess participants' attitudes toward each of two different instructional approaches they received. It repeatedly has been established as a reliable evaluative instrument (see appendix A).

What Does the Research Say?

Pizzo originally designed this assessment to compare the attitudes of students toward acoustical environmental conditions that either were matched or mismatched with their learning-style preferences for sound. According to Hodges (1985), seventh- and eighth-grade students who were taught and tested in their preferred formal or informal seating design demonstrated statistically more positive attitudes than those in mismatched conditions. Martini (1986) used the SDS to assess the attitudes of auditory-, tactual-, and visual-preferenced middle-school students toward congruent and incongruent instructional strategies in order to compare the relative effectiveness of perceptually responsive and perceptually dissonant instructional resources. DeBello (1985) examined the sociological implications of eighth-grade students learning individually, in pairs, in a group, and with their teacher. The results showed significantly higher attitude-test scores when composition revision strategies were congruent, rather than incongruent, with their preferences. According to Garrett (1991), matching, rather than mismatching, individual perceptual preferences with instructional methods statistically increased high-school students' attitude-test scores toward learning vocabulary. Crossley (2007) compared middle school ELL students' attitudes toward learning traditionally versus learning with an MIP by administering the SDS.

Comparing Attitudes toward Three or More Different Treatments

When we are interested in which method or resource most students prefer when we have exposed them to three or more different treatments, we use the Comparative Value Scale (CVS) (O'Connell, 2000; Perna, 2007; Roberts, 2004–2005) (see appendix B). The CVS includes 12 bipolar descriptive pairs that, for example, measure students' attitudes toward learning new and difficult vocabulary words through three different methods—traditional teaching versus tactual resources versus kinesthetic resources. The CVS was administered when teaching high school students science traditionally versus with teacher-created tactual and kinesthetic materials, versus with student-created tactual and kinesthetic materials (O'Connell, 1999). Roberts (2004–2005) administered it to middle school youth studying science.

Students rate their attitudes toward three or more treatments by identifying how they feel about learning on a five-point Likert-type scale. Choices for each question include a range from each method being "very helpful" to "not helpful at all." In each of the 12 questions, students are asked to compare two of the three (or more) methods through which they were taught. Three questions pertain to how well each method helped them in the following categories: Learning the New Material; Remembering the New Material; Enjoying the New Material; and Understanding the New Material.

ASSESSING LEARNING-STYLE IMPLEMENTATION

Dunn and Burke (2000) designed an easy-to-use assessment to gather evidence about learning-style implementation. The tool was originally intended as a supervisory scale; however, we suggest that teachers or teams of teachers use this instrument as a planning/self-assessment measure. Observers merely need to see whether specific items are present in the classroom, such as tactual materials. They either are there or they are not. If they are present, are they correct? If they are correct, have they been used? Are there enough for everyone on the roster? (See appendix C.)

EXPERIMENTING WITH LEARNING-STYLE INSTRUCTIONAL STRATEGIES

Whenever students begin to lag behind their class counterparts, experiment with one of the instructional strategies described in this book—CAPs, PLSs, MIPs, Small-Group Strategies, or Tactual or Kinesthetic Resources. Apply the descriptions of the learning-style traits that respond to each of the strategies for choosing the new method you will try. Establish clear, concise objectives for each lesson and test to those objectives. Teach two or more lessons with whichever new strategy that you decide to implement. Compare the gains the at-risk students make with the new approach we have suggested against whichever method you used previously. If they do achieve better, use either the SDS or the CVC to compare their attitudes toward the new versus the previous method. Such data present clear guidelines concerning how individuals with different learning styles should be taught.

BACK TO THE BEGINNING

We don't know which of these suggestions the three, fourth-grade teachers would decide to use, but based on the reports from all over the United States (Dunn & DeBello, 1999), we are confident that they will be very pleased with the outcomes as shown through their students' higher achievement, improved attitudes toward school, and better behavior.

The incremental process described in this chapter indicates how teachers and administrators can move forward toward beginning learning-style-based instruction. It also describes what is likely to occur when students are taught with learning-style responsive instruction. We owe children nothing less.

REFLECTION POINTS:

1. Consider the following quote from Bennett (2003). In which ways could you use this argument when implementing learning styles with your at-risk students?

   "The concept of learning styles offers a value-neutral approach for understanding individual differences among ethnically different students and within any group. . . . The assumption is that everyone can learn, provided teachers respond appropriately to individual learning needs" (p. 187).

2. Plan a parent-teacher information meeting. How would you introduce learning styles to the parents in your class or building? How would you help them recognize the need for differentiating instruction in the classroom? What advice would you give them for helping their child to learn at home?

Chapter Twelve

Research on the Dunn and Dunn Learning-Styles Model: How Do We Know It Works?

Learning style is a biologically and developmentally determined set of unique characteristics that make the identical instruction effective for some students and ineffective for others. Although initially conceived as an outgrowth of practitioners' observations, this model's roots can be traced to two distinct theories—cognitive-style theory and brain lateralization theory.

Cognitive-style theory indicates that individuals process information differently on the basis of both learned and inherent traits. To gain information in that arena, many previous researchers investigated the variables of field dependence/independence, global/analytic, simultaneous/successive, and/or left- or right-preference processing. As they sought to determine whether relationships existed among these cognitive dimensions and students' environmental, emotional, sociological, and physiological traits, they found that certain variables often clustered together.

RELATIONSHIPS BETWEEN COGNITIVE STYLE AND LEARNING STYLE

Relationships exist between learning persistently (with few or no interspersed relaxation or reflection periods), in a quiet, well-lit environment, in formal seating, with little or no intake, and analytic *left* processing. Similarly, students with comparatively short attention spans and who feel most comfortable in soft illumination, with several breaks, informal seating, and snacks often reveal high scores as global *right* processors (Dunn et al., 1990; Dunn, Cavanaugh et al., 1982; Guastello & Burke, 1998–1999). Furthermore, field dependence/independence correlates in many ways with a global/analytic cognitive style and elicits the same clustering as right- and left-preferenced students (Brennan, 1982; Douglas, 1979; Levy, 1982; Trautman, 1979; Zenhausern, 1982).

In some cases, more attributes ally themselves with global/right tendencies than with their counterparts. Thus, although global/rights often enjoy working with peers and using tactual resources, analytic/lefts do not manifest the reverse preferences; nor are their sociological or perceptual characteristics similar (Dunn, Cavanaugh et al., 1982).

BRAIN LATERALIZATION THEORY

As the relationships among various cognitive-style theories became evident, brain lateralization theory emerged based, to a large extent, on the writing of Paul Broca, whose research led him to propose that the two hemispheres of the human brain have different functions. Subsequent research by the Russian scientist Alexander Luria (1973) and the American scientist, Roger Sperry (who received a Nobel prize for his split-brain experiments in 1981), demonstrated that the left hemisphere appeared to be associated with verbal and sequential abilities, whereas the right hemisphere appeared to be associated with emotions and spatial, holistic processing. Those conclusions, however, continue to be challenged. Nevertheless, it is clear that people begin to concentrate, process, and remember in very different patterns. Thus, the Dunn and Dunn Learning-Styles Model is based on decades of research that substantiates that:

1. most individuals can learn;
2. instructional environments, resources, and approaches respond to diverse learning-style strengths;
3. most people have strengths, but different people have very different strengths;
4. individual instructional preferences exist and can be measured reliably (www.learningstyles.net);
5. given responsive environments, resources, and approaches, students attain statistically higher achievement and attitude test scores in congruent, rather than in incongruent treatments (Dunn & DeBello, 1999; Dunn & Dunn, 1992, 1993; Dunn et al., 1994; Dunn & Griggs, 2007b). They also behave better in style-responsive environments (Fine, 2003; Oberer, 1999, 2003);
6. most teachers can learn to use learning styles (Dunn & Dunn, 1999);
7. most students can learn to capitalize on their learning-style strengths when concentrating on new and difficult information (Dunn, 2001).

WHAT MAKES THIS MODEL UNIQUE?

During the past 40 years, this model has been developed, researched, refined, and used experimentally to examine many instructional practices in both congruent and incongruent treatments for students with diverse learning styles (Dunn, Thies, & Honigsfeld, 2001; Lovelace, 2005). This model:

- identifies the learning-style profile of students in kindergarten through adulthood with age-compatible assessments (www.learningstyles.net);
- provides the first globally formatted learning-style instruments for elementary, middle-school, high-school, and adult learners (www.learningstyles.net);
- provides compatible learning-style prescriptions for how each student should study and do homework (Brand, 1999; Carns & Carns, 1991; Clark-Thayer, 1987; Cook, 1989; Dunn & Griggs, 1988; Geiser, 1999; Lenehan, 1994; Lenehan et al., 1994; Marino, 1993; Minotti, 2002; Monsour, 1991; Nelson, 1991; Nelson, Dunn, Griggs, Primavera, Fitzpatrick, Bacilious et al., 1993; Ogden, 1989; Raviotta, 1989; Turner, 1992; White, 1996);
- has been field-tested nationally with multiple instructional approaches for teaching identical subject-matter to students with unique learning-style strengths (Dunn & Griggs, 2007b).
- has been utilized and analyzed by researchers at more than 350 institutions of higher education (Dunn & Griggs, 2007b; also see www.learningstyles.net);
- has been implemented throughout the United States (Dunn & DeBello, 1999) and in at least 30 nations internationally (Boström & Schmidt, 2006; Brunner & Dunn, 1997; Dunn, Griggs, Milgram, & Price, 1997–1998; Buli-Holmberg et al., 2007; Milgram, Dunn, & Price, 1993; also see www.learningstyles.net). Specifically, research projects were conducted in:
    1. Australia (Murray-Harvey, 1994);
    2. the Bahamas (Roberts, 1984);
    3. Bermuda (Bascome, 2004; Bassett, 2004; DeShields, 2005; Honigsfeld & Lister, 2003; Landy, 2005; Lister, 2004; Ming, 2004; Roberts, 2004–2005; Tully, 2004; Tully, Dunn, & Hlawaty, 2006);
    4. Brazil (DePaula, 2002, 2007; Wechsler, 1993);
    5. Brunei (Pengiran-Jadid, 1998, 2003, 2004, 2007);
    6. Canada (Brodhead & Price, 1993; Mariash, 1983);
    7. the former Czechoslovakia (Karlova, Lekarska, & Kralove, 1994);
    8. Denmark (Boström & Schmidt, 2006);
    9. Egypt (Soliman, 1993);
    10. Germany (Hlawaty, 2002, 2003, 2004, 2007);

11. Greece (Spiridakis, 1993);
12. Guatemala (Sinatra, Sazo de Mendez, & Price, 1993);
13. Honduras (DiSebastian, 1994);
14. Hungary (Honigsfeld, 2000, 2001, 2003a, 2004, 2007);
15. Israel (Milgram, Dunn, & Price, 1993; Shemer, 1995);
16. Jamaica (Roberts, 1984);
17. Korea (Hong, Milgram, & Perkins, 1995; Hong & Suh, 1995; Suh & Price, 1993);
18. Malaysia (Lau, 1997);
19. Mexico (Ingham, Ponce Meza, & Price, 1998);
20. New Zealand (Honigsfeld & Cooper, 2003, 2004, 2007);
21. Norway (Buli-Holmberg et al., 2007;
22. the Philippines (Ingham, 1989; Ingham & Price, 1993; Li, 1989; Orden, 2004; Orden & Querol, 2005; Orden & Ramos, 2005);
23. Puerto Rico (Ramirez, 1982; Vazquez, 1985);
24. Russia (Ulubabova, 2003, 2004, 2007);
25. Singapore (Lam-Phoon, 1986; Yeap, 1987);
26. South Africa (Nganwa-Bagumah & Mwamwenda, 1991);
27. Sweden (Boström, 2004; Bostrom & Kroksmark, 2005; Boström & Lassen, 2006; Calissendorff, 2006; Honigsfeld & Gard, 2003);
29. Taiwan (Chen, 2005; Chiu, 1993; Lo, 1994); and
30. the United States (Dunn & Griggs, 2003, 2004, 2007a).

Research on this model has contributed to our expanding knowledge of learning styles and brain behavior. "It has given the world a fundamental new tool that provides a deeper and more profound view of the learner than previously perceived" (Keefe, 1982, Foreword, p. 1).

RESEARCH ON THE DUNN AND DUNN LEARNING-STYLES MODEL

Practitioners' Findings

It has become common practice for practitioners using Dunn and Dunn learning-style approaches to report statistically improved standardized achievement- and attitude-test scores among poorly achieving and special education students. Such data were published for elementary through high-school students in urban, suburban, and rural schools across the nation by supervisors of varied backgrounds and experiences, and with learners so diverse that they defy categorization (Andrews, 1990; Bauer, 1987, 1991; Dunn & Dunn, 2008; Elliot, 1991; Favre, 2003; Fine, 2002, 2003; Gadwa & Griggs, 1985;

Klavas, 1991; Neely & Alm, 1992, 1993; Orsak, 1990; Perrin, 1990; Stone, 1992; Wood, 2002; also see www.learningstyles.net).

According to the Center for Research in Education (CRE), the 20-year period of extensive federal funding between 1970 and 1990 produced very few programs that resulted in significantly higher standardized achievement test scores for special education students (Alberg, Cook, Fiore, Friend, Sano, Lillie et al., 1992). When that four-year, federal government study concluded its interviews, multiple visits to school sites, and extensive examination of school data, its staff reported that, prominent among those programs that did demonstrate statistically higher standardized achievement test scores, was the Dunn and Dunn Learning-Styles Model.

Researchers' Findings

Research on the Dunn and Dunn model was conducted at more than 135 institutions of higher education and included more than 850 studies, monographs, and other publications (see www.learningstyles.net). It provides extensive data concerning the learning styles of different achievement, age, gender, national, and brain-processing groups. It reveals how, on the basis of learning-style strengths, individuals can be taught to absorb and retain new and difficult academic information and which approaches, methods, and resources are most likely to be effective for whom. It also demonstrates that traditional instruction is the *least* effective way of teaching nontraditional learners—most of whom tend to be global processors with tactual, kinesthetic, or verbal/kinesthetic strengths who need mobility while concentrating. Such children tend to be low auditory, low visual, collegial, and nonauthority oriented, and often are in need of mobility, relaxation breaks, low illumination, music or discussions, and snacks while learning.

HOW DO LEARNING STYLES DIFFER AMONG STUDENTS?

Learning styles vary by (a) age, (b) achievement level, (c) gender, (d) global versus analytic processing, and (e) nation (Dunn & Griggs, 2007b). Dunn and Griggs (1998) reviewed studies of multiculturally diverse students in the United States and reported that so many styles existed *within each group* that there were more within-group than between-group differences. In the same family, mothers and fathers usually had diametrically opposite learning styles and their first two offspring rarely learned in the same way (Borchetta, 2007; Leone, 2008).

Differences by Achievement

Individuals' learning styles also differ by high- versus low-academic achievement. Although many gifted students learn differently from each other and underachievers have a variety of learning-style attributes, gifted and underachieving students have significantly different learning styles and are unlikely to perform well with the same methods (Dunn, 2002; Dunn & Griggs, 2007b; Favre, 2003; Fine, 2002, 2003; Levine, 2007). Conversely, gifted students in nine diverse cultures with talents in athletics, art, dance, leadership, literature, mathematics, or music, evidenced essentially similar learning-style characteristics to other students with the same talent (Milgram et al., 1993).

Differences by Gender

Individuals' learning styles differ by gender (Dunn & Griggs, 2007b; Honigsfeld & Dunn, 2003; Reese & Dunn, 2007–2008). Many males and females frequently learn differently from each other. Males tend to be more kinesthetic, tactual, and visual, and need more mobility in a more informal environment than females. Males also are more nonconforming and peer motivated than their female classmates.

More females than males tend to be auditory and internally, authority, and parent motivated, and better able to sit passively in conventional classroom desks and chairs than males. Females also tend to (a) need significantly more quiet while learning (Pizzo, Dunn, & Dunn, 1990) and (b) be more conforming than males (Marcus, 1977). Although some people believe that societal mores may be responsible for the higher conformity levels of females, in every nation in which we compared secondary students by gender, girls were more academically conforming, motivated, and persistent than boys (Dunn & Griggs, 2007b). In effect, those data tend to support Restak's (1979) and Thies's (1979, 1999–2000) conclusions concerning the influence of biology on learning style.

Hormones as a Possible Basis for Gender Learning Differences

More recently, scientific attention has been focused on hormones, one of the regulatory systems influencing brain cognition, emotions, and behavior in humans and animals. Sex hormones influence prenatal brain structures to prepare targeted neuronal circuits for activation during and after puberty. Testosterone is believed to affect cognition and thinking in humans as well as sex differences in cognitive abilities. Indeed, scientists have been investigating associations between testosterone and different levels of intelligence in young prepubertal children of both sexes.

Differences by Age

Learning styles occasionally change as individuals grow older (Dunn & Griggs, 1998). In particular, children's perceptual strengths often change between primary and elementary school, between elementary and middle school, and between middle school and secondary school. Learning style can change throughout the school years and may continue to do so in college and during adulthood (Dunn & Griggs, 1998; Price, 1980; Van Wynen, 1999, 2001). However, individuals change uniquely. Although many patterns exist, some people barely change at all and others experience rapid and multiple changes. Nevertheless, it is possible to anticipate approximate achievement and behavioral levels by merely knowing the age, gender, and learning styles of students in an incoming class.

Differences by Sociological Preferences

Sociological preferences for learning either alone, with peers, with an authoritative versus a collegial teacher, and/or with routines and patterns as opposed to in a variety of social groupings develop over time, change with age and maturity, and are considered developmental (Dunn & Griggs, 1998; Thies, 1979). Young children tend to begin school highly parent, teacher, and/or adult motivated. Many become peer motivated by fifth or sixth grade and remain that way until approximately ninth grade, when they often become self-motivated. Gifted children tend to become self-motivated early—frequently by first or second grade—and rarely experience a strongly peer-motivated stage. Underachievers become peer motivated earlier than average students and tend to remain that way longer—often well past adolescence.

Differences by Emotional Preferences

Motivation, responsibility (conformity versus nonconformity), and the need for internal versus external structure are perceived as being developmental (Thies, 1979, 1999–2000). Motivation fluctuates day to day, class to class, and teacher to teacher. However, many people appear to experience at least three stages of nonconformity that tend to correlate with high and low *responsibility* levels (Dunn, White, & Zenhausern, 1982).

The first period of nonconformity occurs for many between the first and second years of life. In the United States, this first stage euphemistically is called the "terrible twos" and coincides with children beginning the pattern of resisting adult directives. For most children this first stage of nonconformity lasts for less than a year.

The second period of nonconformity often begins at about sixth grade and tends to linger until ninth or tenth grade for many average children. Some remain nonconforming until well past high school and others into adulthood. Gifted students often are among the most nonconforming youth; they invariably perceive things their own way.

Differences by Perceptual Preferences

The younger the children, the more tactual (learning by handling and manipulating instructional resources) and/or kinesthetic (learning by active involvement and experience) their perceptual strengths are likely to be. Less than 12% of elementary school children are *auditory* learners—meaning that they are capable of remembering at least 75% of the academic information they listen to for 30–40 minutes. Less than 40% are *visual* learners; few children or adults are capable of remembering at least 75% of what they read in 30–40 minutes. Usually, the older the children, the more their auditory and visual modalities have developed. However, many high school males are neither auditory nor visual learners; they remain essentially tactual or kinesthetic throughout their lives.

Low- and average-achieving students earn statistically higher scores on achievement and attitude tests when taught through tactual/visual and kinesthetic/visual instructional resources—as opposed to when taught through auditory/visual approaches. Even adult teachers learned more, more quickly, and retained it better in learning-style-responsive programs than in traditional staff development (Raupers, 1999; Taylor, 1999). Teachers also enjoyed learning more in responsive rather than in dissonant staff-development sessions (Scricca, 2007).

Forty years ago, educators knew little about tactual or kinesthetic learners. During the past quarter of a century, many researchers have documented the existence and potency of perceptual preferences for at-risk students. We recently have probed another type of modality—the verbal kinesthetic person. These are people who internalize more quickly and efficiently when they *talk about* what they are hearing while they listen. In effect, they do not absorb new and difficult information unless they talk about it while someone else is speaking. If this phenomenon seems strange, that is exactly how most of us felt almost 30 years ago when Carbo (1980), Urbschat (1977), and Wheeler (1983) found that some children do not absorb what they hear and others do not retain what they see. Today, we recognize those learners almost immediately.

Differences by Processing Styles

Individuals differ in how they absorb and process new and difficult information. Investigations of global versus analytic and/or left- versus right-preferences revealed that: (a) relationships exist among these cognitive dimensions and many students' environmental, emotional, sociological, and/or physiological learning-style traits and (b) these cognitive dimensions and specific learning-style traits often cluster together. For example, learning persistently (with few or no intermissions), in a quiet, well-lit, formal setting with little or no intake, often correlates with being an analytic or left processor. Conversely, learning with intermittent periods of concentration and relaxation, in soft lighting and with sound (music or voices), while seated informally and snacking, often correlates with highly global- or right-processing styles (Cody 1983; Dunn, Bruno et al., 1990; Dunn, Cavanaugh et al., 1982). In some cases, attributes ally themselves with one processing style more than another. Although global and right-preferenced students often prefer learning tactually and with peers (Jarsonbeck, 1984), no clear perceptual or social pattern has been revealed by analytic or left-preferenced students.

Many researchers revealed the effects of sequential versus simultaneous instructional approaches on identified analytic and global students (Brennan, 1984; Douglas, 1979; Dunn, Cavanaugh et al., 1982; Dunn, Bruno et al., 1990; Orazio, 1999; Tanenbaum, 1982; Trautman, 1979). Those early researchers found that analytic students who were taught analytically, and global students who were taught globally, achieved statistically higher achievement-test scores than they did with dissonant instructional strategies. That occurred in high-school biology (Douglas, 1979), mathematics (Brennan, 1984), and nutrition (Tanenbaum, 1982), in junior-high school mathematics (Orazio, 1999) and social studies (Trautman, 1979), and in community-college mathematics (Dunn, Bruno et al., 1990).

Orazio (1999) reported that almost all average- and well-achieving seventh-grade adolescents performed statistically ($p < .001$) better on mathematics achievement tests with global rather than with analytic teaching approaches. Only the extreme analytics (approximately 10–12% of the population) performed better ($p < .001$) with analytic than with global instructional strategies.

On the basis of years of experimentation, we believe that approximately 85% of elementary school students and 55% of adult learners are global. Seventeen percent of the adults we have tested appear to be integrated, and 28% of normally functioning adults seem to be analytic. Those percentages vary by achievement and age. More analytics are high achievers, but the majority of middle-school students seem to be global (Sagan, 2002). Nevertheless, traditional teaching tends to be analytic—fact after fact, progressing from one detail to the next, and gradually building toward an understanding. Therefore, it is not surprising that global students often find conventional teaching difficult to absorb, uninteresting, and far from stimulating.

CONTRASTING RESULTS BETWEEN LEARNING-STYLE AND SPECIAL-EDUCATION PRACTICES

Given (a) the extensive research published during the past four decades, (b) widespread practitioners' reports documenting the reversal of poor school achievement after learning-style-responsive strategies were substituted for traditional teaching, and (c) our expanding knowledge of individuals' unique characteristics, it seems apparent that effective teaching requires the adoption of a variety of instructional approaches for students who either do not learn—or do not like learning—conventionally. Educators, counselors, parents, psychologists, and students need to recognize that individual learning style should be the basis of many educational decisions—assignments to classes, groups, resources, or teachers, and even the time of day when students are taught or tested.

This departure from tradition is particularly justified in light of educators' egregious track record with special education (SPED) students, such as in New York City. Since 1975, the number of the city's SPED students rose from 35,000 to 167,000—nearly 15% of the city's 1.1 million students. Worse than the increase in numbers, is the fact that most classified SPED students in that, and every other, urban center rarely outgrow that denigrating designation. Less than 2% are released from the SPED category each year; 97–98% remain so classified. Very clearly, the billions of dollars allocated to the SPED bureaucracy have been ineffective with 98% of the students (Edelman, 1998).

Contrast these New York City results with those of Buffalo, the second-largest urban center in New York State. Under the supervision of a team of researchers from the State University of New York at Buffalo, classified

Table 12.1. Comparisons of Standardized Achievement Test Scores in Reading and Mathematics between Students Participating in a Learning-Styles (LS) Program and a Non-learning Styles (Non-LS) Program.

Test	*Group*	*Pretest*	*Posttest*	*Difference*
Reading (WJ)	LS	72.38	79.10	+6.72
	Non-LS	76.48	71.52	−4.96
Math (WJ)	LS	69.67	84.20	+14.53
	Non-LS	73.52	69.09	−4.43
Reading (CTBS)	LS	18.76	31.33	+12.57
	Non-LS	24.83	21.25	−3.58
Math (CTBS)	LS	15.83	18.61	+2.78
	Non-LS	23.44	16.95	−6.49

Learning Disabled (LD) and Emotionally Handicapped (EH) students in the Buffalo City Schools were randomly selected and randomly assigned to two groups. The experimental group capitalized on students' individual learning styles; students taught themselves and each other with tactual and kinesthetic resources. The control group was taught with conventional lectures, discussions, readings, and writings by their certified, experienced SPED teachers.

Results at the end of two years revealed that the experimental group achieved statistically higher test scores than the control group in *both reading and mathematics* on two different standardized achievement tests—the Woodcock-Johnson (WJ) and the California Tests of Basic Skills (CTBS). In contrast, the control group evidenced academic *losses* between the pretest and posttest (Dunn & DeBello, 1999; Quinn, 1993) (see table 12.1).

The Buffalo findings revealed that LD and EH students whose instruction was not responsive to their learning styles achieved significantly less well than LD and EH students whose instruction was responsive to their learning styles. Nothing differed between the experimental and control groups other than the learning-styles instruction with which they were taught. Based on these data, it seems reasonable to conjecture that LD students have been mislabeled. As we stated at the end of chapter 1, it is more likely that they are teaching disabled (TD).

REFLECTION POINTS

1. Review the following list of statements and consider whether you agree (A) or disagree (D) with each. If possible, have a colleague do the same and then compare and discuss your answers.
   1 Learning preferences and learning styles often are used interchangeably.
   2. Professional teachers understand the importance of helping all their students learn how to learn.
   3. A learning style is a set of biological and developmental characteristics.
   4. Learning style is just another fad that will fade in a couple of years.
   5. There are more than 30 different learning-style models.
   6. There is no "scientifically based research" on learning styles.
   7. There are no gender differences between the learning styles of boys and girls.
   8. Learning style does not remain stable over time.

9. Each culture has a specific, well-defined set of learning-style characteristics.

See upside-down below.

2. As adults, teachers have their own unique learning styles. Think of times when you chose to use your own learning-style strengths as a teacher. Think of ways for teachers to capitalize on their strengths while simultaneously teaching students with diverse learning-style traits.

The authors' answers to the statements in Question 1:
1. A, 2. A, 3. A, 4. D, 5. A, 6. D, 7. D, 8. A, 9., D

Chapter Thirteen

How Schools, Parents, and Courts Can Respond to Federal Law and Improve Classroom Teaching for At-Risk Students

Robin A. Boyle

As the title of this book suggests, its chapters address a variety of strategies for teaching at-risk students—those who are both classified and those who are considered borderline in terms of performance in school. The law, unfortunately, provides procedures and assistance for only those who are officially classified as learning disabled, and not for the larger category of at-risk students. Therefore, our legal framework for teaching at-risk students needs further expansion. It is our strong belief that the U.S. federal legislature, courts, and schools should strive to facilitate a working definition of *learning styles*.

The research on learning styles indicates that many officially classified at-risk students are those who are very global, tactual, and kinesthetic; they also may be peer oriented (socially inclined). These students may be very intelligent and quite capable of mastering academic material, but when the primary method of teaching is geared toward learning styles very different from theirs, their brilliance and aptitude for success are less apparent and teachers perceive them as poor performers. Students who achieve well in traditional schools tend to be analytic, auditory, and authority oriented in their learning styles; they are typically rewarded with higher grades than those who become at risk. As this book has demonstrated in its instructional chapters, when global, tactual, and kinesthetic students are taught in ways that complement their learning styles, they can and do succeed academically (Dunn & DeBello, 1999). It is morally inappropriate to teach all students the same way, given the diversity of learning styles in any classroom. Where

Note to Readers: The citation form used in this chapter is in the proper legal citation form. *Id.* refers the reader to the preceding cited authority. Furthermore, statutes have sections and are abbreviated as "Sec."

untapped chances of success abound with at-risk students, the law needs to address current instructional deficiencies.

OUR FEDERAL LAWS

In 1990, Congress provided our country with a landmark legal reform when it incorporated the Education for All Handicapped Children Act of 1975 (Pub. L. 94-142, 89 Stat. 773), into the Individuals with Disabilities in Education Act (IDEA) (20 U.S.C. Sec. 1400 et seq). Declaring that the former laws needed revision because the needs of "millions of children with disabilities were not being fully met," Congress declared that:

> Disability is a natural part of the human experience and in no way diminishes the right of individuals to participate in or contribute to society. Improving educational results for children with disabilities is an essential element of our national policy of ensuring equality of opportunity, full participation, independent living, and economic self-sufficiency for individuals with disabilities. (Sec. 1400)

To meet these goals, Congress perceived it valuable for teachers and schools to "improve the academic achievement and functional performance of children with disabilities, including the use of scientifically based instructional practices, to the maximum extent possible." *Id.* Given the plethora of empirical research studies documented in this book, the question arises whether our schools have provided sufficient *scientifically based* teaching methods to reach at-risk students. As discussed in the earlier chapters of this book, studies have demonstrated that students who either are classified as learning disabled or are generally perceived as at-risk demonstrate academic success when instructional methods complement their learning styles. Thus different instructional strategies are warranted to reach at-risk students.

When unveiling its new legislation, Congress further declared that, "it is in the national interest that the Federal Government have a supporting role in assisting State and local efforts to educate children with disabilities in order to improve results for such children and to ensure *equal protection of the law*." *Id.* (emphasis added). The research and teaching methods provided in this book beg the question as to whether at-risk students are being provided equal protection under the law.

The IDEA provides that "all children with disabilities have available to them a free appropriate public education [FAPE] that emphasizes special education and related services designed to meet their unique needs." *Id.* To achieve a FAPE, Congress announced "that educators and parents have the necessary tools to improve educational results for children with disabilities by supporting system improvement activities, coordinated research, and personnel preparation." *Id.* Given this Congressional mandate, school administrators should ask whether their teachers are receiving sufficient education in their graduate education classes as to the research findings regarding learning styles. Have our schools ensured that teachers receive continuing education? Are our local, state, and federal systems meeting the standards of a FAPE that meets the unique needs of our students?

The process for obtaining school assistance in teaching disabled students begins with an "individualized education plan" (IEP) tailored to the disabled child's unique needs (20 U.S.C. Sec. 1414 [2005]). The IEP is a written statement, developed at a meeting of the school administrators, the teacher, and the parents. At this meeting, what will be considered in developing the IEP will be the child's current performance, the goals and short-term instructional objectives, the specific educational services offered, and the criteria and evaluation procedures used to determine whether the objectives are being achieved. The "IDEA does not require that a school either maximize a student's potential or provide the best education at public expense" *Fort Zumwalt School Dist. v. Clynes* (119 F.3d 607, 612 [8th Cir. 1997]). Rather, the United States Supreme Court pronounced the standard to be that a school district satisfies its obligations under IDEA if (a) it complies with the act's procedural requirements and (b) the IEP is "*reasonably calculated* to enable the child to receive educational benefits" (*Board of Educ. v. Rowley*, 458 U.S. 176, 206-07 [1982]) (emphasis added). In expressing this standard, the Court held that the act does not require the state to "maximize the potential of each handicapped child commensurate with the opportunity provided non-handicapped children." *Id.* at 200. Considering that there is ample empirical evidence demonstrating the potential success of teaching at-risk students, perhaps courts should consider that schools be held accountable to a higher standard for teaching these low-performing students.

Although students' learning styles and individual abilities at one time played a role in the development of the IEPs, they are playing less of a role since the 2004 amendments to the IDEA. Currently, the 2001 No Child Left Behind Act (Pub. L. 107-110, 115 Stat. 1425, and incorporated as 20 U.S.C.A. Sec. 6301 et seq.), has influenced procedures under the IDEA to the extent that there has been more of an emphasis lately on students' performance on standardized tests. The act's purpose is "to ensure that all children have a fair, equal, and significant opportunity to obtain a high-quality education and reach, at a minimum, proficiency on challenging State academic achievement standards and state academic assessments" (Sec. 6301).

Despite the rise in concern over standardized test scores, parents, students, and educators should strive to include within their IEP's a working definition of learning styles. In reviewing case decisions, it appears that not all school districts and courts are using the term correctly or even similarly. As defined by the Dunn and Dunn model, learning style is "the way in which an individual begins to concentrate on, process, internalize, and remember new and difficult academic information or skills" (Dunn & Dunn, 1993, p. 2). When all pertinent parties to the IEP agree on the working definition of learning styles, there should follow an assessment of each student's individual learning style. The assessment that these authors recommend varies for the age of each student, but each can be accessed at www.learningstyles.net.

Having the relevant information regarding the student's learning style, in addition to the individualized profile that each assessment generates, the school administrators, parents, and students would be better able to develop an effective IEP. The IEPs should include instructional strategies describing how teachers can best teach to each particular student's learning-style strengths. Older students can develop strategies for teaching themselves via their own learning style's characteristics. Parents of younger students also can develop strategies concerning how to translate classroom materials into individualized homework instruction for their children. For at-risk students who are not classified as *disabled*, and, therefore, the procedures of writing an IEP do not necessarily apply, the learning-style assessments would be a good starting point for putting together in-depth study suggestions for at-risk students.

Courts, schools, and parents are advised to use the various learning-style identification assessments and the working definition of learning styles when formulating instructional strategies for all students experiencing academic difficulty. The current federal statute, IDEA, and the most recent United States Supreme Court case ruling currently do not hold schools accountable to a standard commensurate with what at-risk students are capable of achieving when they are taught in ways that complement their learning styles. We firmly believe that professional, state-certified educational institutions should be accountable for the extent to which they attempt to maximize student academic potential based on attention to how each child learns.

REFLECTION POINTS

1. With a group of colleagues, discuss your experiences that would support the claim that "our legal framework for teaching at-risk students needs further expansion."
2. Review the IEP of one of your students. In which way(s) does it address and in which way(s) could it be improved to address your students' learning-styles needs better?

Appendix A: Semantic Differential Scale (SDS) (Pizzo, 1981)

MY REACTIONS TO STUDYING THROUGH LEARNING-STYLE STRATEGIES

Directions: Place an X in one of the five spaces in between the pairs of opposite-meaning words. Choose the space closest to the word on each line that indicates your reaction to learning with the learning-style strategies.

For example, if you felt that the strategy you used confused you, indicate the following:

CONFUSED _X_: ___: ___: ___: ___ CLEAR-MINDED

In contrast, if you believe the strategy you used helped you study, indicate the following:

CONFUSED ___: ___: ___: ___: _X_ CLEAR-MINDED

A check in the middle space indicates a neutral reaction, which means you don't have feelings to report:

CONFUSED ___: ___: _X_: ___: ___ CLEAR-MINDED

Begin here:

HELPFUL	___: ___: ___: ___: ___	NOT HELPFUL
ENERGETIC	___: ___: ___: ___: ___	TIRED
UNEASY	___: ___: ___: ___: ___	COMFORTABLE
DETERMINED	___: ___: ___: ___: ___	INADEQUATE
ANXIOUS	___: ___: ___: ___: ___	STRESS-FREE

WONDERFUL	___: ___: ___: ___: ___	TERRIBLE
UNSTEADY	___: ___: ___: ___: ___	SECURE
CONFIDENT	___: ___: ___: ___: ___	UNCERTAIN
BAD	___: ___: ___: ___: ___	GOOD
UNDISTURBED	___: ___: ___: ___: ___	BOTHERED
DULL	___: ___: ___: ___: ___	SHARP
UNSUCCESSFUL	___: ___: ___: ___: ___	SUCCESSFUL

Appendix B: Comparative Values Scale (O'Connell, 2000)

Answer each of the following questions giving the **highest** rating to the method that helped you learn **best** and the **lowest** rating to the method that helped you learn least.

1. Compared with the lessons in which your **teacher wrote on the board and distributed dittos and notes,** how beneficial in helping you **LEARN** the science requirements were the lessons in which the **TEACHER** made Fact Fans, Pic-A-Holes, Floor Games for you?

Very Helpful	Somewhat Helpful	Neutral	Somewhat NOT Helpful	NOT Helpful

2. Compared with the lessons in which your **teacher wrote on the board and distributed dittos and notes,** how beneficial in helping you **LEARN** the science requirements were the lessons in which **YOU made Fact Fans, Pic-A-Holes, and Floor Games**?

Very Helpful	Somewhat Helpful	Neutral	Somewhat NOT Helpful	NOT Helpful

3. Compared with the lessons in which your **teacher wrote on the board and distributed dittos and notes,** how beneficial in helping you **REMEMBER** the science requirements were the lessons in which the TEACHER made Fact Fans, Pic-A-Holes, Floor Games for you?

Very Helpful	Somewhat Helpful	Neutral	Somewhat NOT Helpful	NOT Helpful

4. Compared with the lessons in which your **teacher wrote on the board and distributed dittos and notes,** how beneficial in helping you **REMEMBER** the science requirements were the lessons in which **YOU made Fact Fans, Pic-A-Holes, and Floor Games**?

Very Helpful	Somewhat Helpful	Neutral	Somewhat NOT Helpful	NOT Helpful

5. Compared with the lessons in which your **teacher wrote on the board and distributed dittos and notes,** how beneficial in helping your **UNDERSTAND** the science requirements were the lessons in which the TEACHER made Fact Fans, Pic-A-Holes, and Floor Games for you?

Very Helpful	Somewhat Helpful	Neutral	Somewhat NOT Helpful	NOT Helpful

6. Compared with the lessons in which your **teacher wrote on the board and distributed dittos and notes,** how beneficial in helping you **UNDERSTAND** the science requirements were the lessons in which **YOU made Fact Fans, Pic-A-Holes, and Floor Games**?

Very Helpful	Somewhat Helpful	Neutral	Somewhat NOT Helpful	NOT Helpful

7. Compared with the lessons in which your **teacher wrote on the board and distributed dittos and notes,** how beneficial in helping you **ENJOY LEARNING** the science requirements were the lessons in which **Your TEACHER made Fact Fans, Pic-A-Holes, and Floor Games**?

Very Helpful	Somewhat Helpful	Neutral	Somewhat NOT Helpful	NOT Helpful

8. Compared with the lessons in which your **teacher wrote on the board and distributed dittos and notes,** how beneficial in helping you **ENJOY LEARNING** the science requirements were the lessons in which **YOU made Fact Fans, Pic-A-Holes, and Floor Games**?

Very Helpful	Somewhat Helpful	Neutral	Somewhat NOT Helpful	NOT Helpful

9. Compared with the lessons in which your **TEACHER** made Fact Fans, Pic-A-Holes, and Floor Games, how beneficial in helping you **LEARN**

the science requirements were the lessons in which **YOU** made Fact Fans, Pic-A-Holes, and Floor Games?

Very Helpful	Somewhat Helpful	Neutral	Somewhat NOT Helpful	NOT Helpful

10. Compared with the lessons in which your **TEACHER** made Fact Fans, Pic-A-Holes, and Floor Games, how beneficial in helping you **REMEMBER** the science requirements were the lessons in which **YOU** made Fact Fans, Pic-A-Holes, and Floor Games?

Very Helpful	Somewhat Helpful	Neutral	Somewhat NOT Helpful	NOT Helpful

11. Compared with the lessons in which your **TEACHER** made Fact Fans, Pic-A-Holes, and Floor Games, how beneficial in helping you **UNDERSTAND** the science requirements were the lessons in which **YOU** made Fact Fans, Pic-A-Holes, and Floor Games?

Very Helpful	Somewhat Helpful	Neutral	Somewhat NOT Helpful	NOT Helpful

12. Compared with the lessons in which your **TEACHER** made Fact Fans, Pic-A-Holes, and Floor Games, how beneficial in helping you **ENJOY LEARNING** the science requirements were the lessons in which **YOU** made Fact Fans, Pic-A-Holes, and Floor Games?

Very Helpful	Somewhat Helpful	Neutral	Somewhat NOT Helpful	NOT Helpful

Appendix C: Supervisory Learning-Style Scale (Dunn & Burke, 2000)

Teacher's Name: ______________________________
Grade: ____________________________________
School: ___________________________________
Approximate Number of Students in Class: ___________

LEARNING-STYLE ASSESSMENT

Is There Evidence of	*Yes*	*No*	*Comments*
LS Testing			
Informing Students			
Informing Parents			
Using the Data			
Homework Rx			
Improved Grades			

ROOM REDESIGN

Is There Evidence of	*Yes*	*No*	*Comments*
Varied Areas			
Varied Lighting			
Formal versus Informal Seating			
Disciplined Mobility			
Appropriate Snacking			
Improved Grades			

VARIED INSTRUCTIONAL RESOURCES

Is There Evidence of	*Yes*	*No*	*Comments*
Small-Group Strategies	Team Learning		
	Circle of Knowledge		
Tactual Resources	Electroboard		
	Flip Chute		
	Pic-A-Hole		
	Task Cards		
	Other(s)		
Kinesthetic Resources			
CAP			
PLS			
Student-Created Resources			

ACHIEVEMENT ASSESSMENTS BASED ON LEARNING-STYLE IMPLEMENTATION

Is There Evidence of	*Yes*	*No*	*Comments*
Homework Assignments			
Projects			
Class Tests			
Standardized Tests			
Research			

GLOBAL VERSUS ANALYTIC (G/A) ACCOMMODATIONS

Is There Evidence of	*Yes*	*No*	*Comments*
G/A Introductions			
G/A Visuals			
G/A Seating			
G/A Assignments			
Cartoons, Humor			
Social Preferences			

Is There Evidence of	*Yes*	*No*	*Comments*
Other LS Features			

Observer _______________ Date _______________

References

Alberg, J. L., Cook, L., Fiore, T., Friend, M., Sano, S., Lillie, D., et. al. (1992). *Educational approaches and program options for integrating students with disabilities: A decision tool.* Triangle Park, NC: Research Triangle Institute.

Andrews, R. H. (1990). The development of a learning styles program in a low socioeconomic, underachieving North Carolina elementary school. *Journal of Reading, Writing, and Learning Disabilities International, 6*, 307–313.

Bascome, G. (2004). Effects of learning-styles instructional resources on short- and long-term vocabulary retention and attitudes of seventh-grade language arts students (Doctoral dissertation, St. John's University, 2004). *Dissertation Abstracts International, 65*(02), 439A.

Bassett, M. (2004). Development of an administrative guide to implementing learning-style based instruction in Bermuda schools. (Doctoral dissertation, St. John's University, 2004). *Dissertation Abstracts International, 65*(06), 2071A.

Bauer, E. (1987). Learning style and the learning disabled: Experimentation with ninth-graders. *The Clearing House, 60,* 206–208.

Bauer, E. (1991). The relationships between and among learning style perceptual preferences, instructional strategies, mathematics achievement, and attitude toward mathematics of learning-disabled and emotionally handicapped students in a suburban junior high school (Doctoral dissertation, St. John's University, 1992). *Dissertation Abstracts International, 53*(06), 1378A.

Bennett, C. (2003). *Comprehensive multicultural education: Theory and practice* (5th ed.). Boston: Allyn & Bacon.

Borchetta, J. (2007). Extent to which learning styles of biological siblings are different from and similar to each other's and their parents'. Ed.D. dissertation, St. John's University (New York), School of Education and Human Services, United States—New York. Retrieved September 17, 2008, from Dissertations & Theses: Full Text database. (Publication No. AAT 3256204).

Boström, L. (2004). Lärande och strategier. [Learning and strategies.] *Didacta Varia, 9*(2), 73–81.

Boström, L., & Kroksmark, T. (2005). Learning and strategies—Tidskrift för lärarutbildning och forskning: Umeå universitet. *Journal of Research in Teacher Education, 4,* 39–49.

Boström, L., & Lassen, L. M. (2006). Unraveling learning, learning styles, learning strategies and meta-cognition. *Education + Training, 48*(2/3), 178–189.

Boström, L., & Schmidt, S. E. (2006). The best way of learning! An introduction for students, parents, teachers, nursery teachers and other interested, to our individual learning styles. Middelfart, Danmark: SIS akademi, Danmarks Laeringsstilscente.

Braio, A., Beasley, T. M., Dunn, R., Quinn, P., & Buchanan, K. (1997). Incremental implementation of learning style strategies among urban low achievers. *Journal of Educational Research, 91,* 15–25.

Brand, S. (1999). Learning-style preferences of second- through sixth-grade students medically diagnosed with attention deficit disorders (Doctoral dissertation, St. John's University, 1999). *Dissertation Abstracts International, 60*(11), 3899A.

Brand, S., Dunn, R., & Greb, F. (2002). Learning styles of students with attention deficit hyperactivity disorder: Who are they and how can we teach them? *The Clearing House, 75*, 268–273.

Brennan, P. K. (1982). Teaching to the whole brain. In *Student Learning Styles and Brain Behavior: Programs, Instrumentation, Research* (pp. 212–213). Reston, VA: National Association of Secondary School Principals.

Brennan, P. K. (1984). An analysis of the relationships among hemispheric preference and analytic/global cognitive style, two elements of learning style, method of instruction, gender, and mathematics achievement of tenth-grade geometry students (Doctoral dissertation, St. John's University, 1985). *Dissertation Abstracts International, 45*(11), 3271A.

Brodhead, M. R., & Price, G. E. (1993). The learning styles of artistically talented adolescents in Canada. In R. M. Milgram, R. Dunn, & G. E. Price (Eds.), *Teaching and counseling gifted and talented adolescents: An international learning style perspective* (pp.186–195). Westport, CT: Praeger.

Brunner, C., & Dunn, R. (1997). Learning styles in overseas schools. In R. Dunn, *Everything you need to successfully implement a learning-styles program: Materials and methods* (pp. 71–81). New Wilmington, PA: Association for the Advancement of International Education.

Brunner, C. E., & Majewski, W. S. (1990). Mildly handicapped students can succeed with learning styles. *Educational Leadership, 48*(2), 21–23.

Buli-Holmberg, J., Guldahl, T., & Jensen, R. (2007). *Refleksjon om opplæring—i et læringsstilperspektiv* [Reflections on learning—A learning-style perspective]. Oslo: N.W. Damm & Søn AS.

Cafferty, E. (1980). An analysis of student performance based upon the degree of match between the educational cognitive style of the teachers and the educational cognitive style of the students (Doctoral dissertation, University of Nebraska). *Dissertation Abstracts International, 41*(07), 2908A.

Calissendorff, M. (2006). Understanding the learning style of pre-school children learning the violin. *Music Education Research, 8*(1), 83–96.

Canfield, A. A., & Lafferty, J. C. (1976). *Learning Style Inventory.* Detroit: Humanics Media.

Carbo, M. A. (1980). An analysis of the relationship between the modality preferences of kindergartners and selected reading treatments as they affect the learning of a basic sight-word vocabulary (Doctoral dissertation, St. John's University, 1980). *Dissertation Abstracts International, 41*(04), 1389A. Recipient: Association for Supervision and Curriculum Development National Award for Best Doctoral Research, 1980.

Carbo, M., Dunn, R., & Dunn K. (1986). *Teaching students to read through their individual learning styles.* Englewood Cliffs, NJ: Prentice-Hall.

Carns, A. W., & Carns, M. R. (1991). Teaching study skills, cognitive strategies, and meta cognitive skills through self-diagnosed learning styles. *The School Counselor, 38,* 341–346.

Chen, H.-T. (2006). Taiwanese adolescent students' achievement in reading and mathematics by age, gender, learning style and socio-economic status (Doctoral dissertation, St. John's University, 2006). *Dissertation Abstracts International, 66*(11), 3872A.

Chiu, M. (1993). *Cross-cultural differences in learning styles of secondary school students in Taiwan and the USA.* Unpublished manuscript, Manhasset Public Schools, Manhasset, New York.

Clark-Thayer, S. (1987). The relationship of the knowledge of student perceived learning style preferences, and study habits and attitudes to achievement of college freshmen in a small urban university (Doctoral dissertation, Boston University, 1987). *Dissertation Abstracts International, 48*(04), 872A.

Cody, C. (1983). Learning styles, including hemispheric dominance: A comparative study of average, gifted, and highly gifted students in grades five through twelve (Doctoral dissertation, Temple University). *Dissertation Abstracts International, 44,* 1631A.

Cook, L. (1989). Relationships among learning style awareness, academic achievement, and locus-of-control of community college students (Doctoral dissertation, University of Florida, 1990). *Dissertation Abstracts International, 51*(03), 687A.

Crosley, H. (2007). Effects of traditional teaching vs a multisensory instructional package on the science achievement and attitudes of English language learner middle-school students and English-speaking middle-school students. Ed.D. dissertation, St. John's University (New York), School of Education and Human Services, United States—New York. Retrieved September 21, 2008, from Dissertations & Theses: Full Text database. (Publication No. AAT 3279263).

Curry, L. (1987). *Integrating concepts of cognitive or learning styles: A review with attention to psychometric standards.* Ottawa, Ontario: Canadian College of Health Services Executives.

DeBello, T. (1985). A critical analysis of the achievement and attitude effects of administrative assignments to social studies writing instruction based on identified, eighth grade students' learning style preferences for learning alone, with peers, or with teachers (Doctoral dissertation, St. John's University, 1985). *Dissertation Abstracts International, 47*(01), 68A.

DeBello, T. (1990). Comparison of eleven major learning styles models: Variables, appropriate populations, validity of instrumentation, and the research behind them. *Journal of Reading, Writing, and Learning Disabilities International, 6,* 203–222.

De Paula, R. M. (2002). Comparative analysis of the learning styles of Brazilian versus other adolescents from diverse nations by age, gender, and academic achievement. Ed.D. dissertation, St. John's University (New York), School of Education and Human Services, United States— New York. Retrieved September 15, 2008, from Dissertations & Theses: Full Text database. (Publication No. AAT 3076078).

De Paula, R. M. (2007). Learning styles of Brazilian adolescents. In R. Dunn & S. A. Griggs (Eds.) *Synthesis of the Dunn and Dunn learning-style model research: Who, what, when, where, and so what?* (pp. 131–135). Jamaica, NY: St. John's University's Center for the Study of Learning and Teaching Styles.

DeShields, B. E. W. (2005). Comparison of the learning styles of nurses and teachers in Bermuda by age, gender, educational level, and professional longevity. (Doctoral dissertation, St. John's University, 2002). *Dissertation Abstracts International, 66*(06), 2101A.

DiSebastian, J. (1994). Learning in style in Teguciagalpa, Honduras. *International Education, 21*(71), 11, 16.

Douglas, C. B. (1979). Making biology easier to understand. *The Biology Teacher 4,* 277–299.

Dunn, R. (1996). *How to implement and supervise a learning-style program.* Alexandria, VA: Association for Supervision and Curriculum Development.

Dunn, R. (Ed.). (2001). *The art of significantly increasing science achievement test scores: Research and practical applications.* Jamaica, NY: St. John's University's Center for the Study of Learning and Teaching Styles.

Dunn, R. (2002). Effects of learning-style strategies on special-education students. *Academic Exchange Quarterly, 6*(4), 206–211.

Dunn, R., & Blake, B. E. (Eds.). (2008). *Teaching every child to read: Innovative and practical strategies for K-8 educators and caretakers.* Lanham, MD: Rowman & Littlefield.

Dunn, R., & Brunner, C. (1997). International misconceptions about learning: Where did they begin? *Inter Ed, 24*(81), 1, 9–11.

Dunn, R., Bruno, J., Sklar, R. I., Zenhausern, R., & Beaudry, J. S. (1990). Effects of matching and mismatching minority developmental college students' hemispheric preferences on mathematics scores. *Journal of Educational Research, 83,* 283–288.

Dunn, R., & Burke, K. (1998). Learning Styles: The Clue to You! www.learningstyles.net.

Dunn, R., & Burke, K. (2000). *Supervisory learning style scale.* Jamaica, NY: St. John's University.

Dunn, R., Cavanaugh, D., Eberle, B., & Zenhausern, R. (1982). Hemispheric preference: The newest element of learning style. *The American Biology Teacher, 44*(5), 291–294.

Dunn, R., & DeBello, T. C. (Eds.) (1999). Improved test scores, attitudes, and behaviors in America's schools: Supervisors' success stories. Westport, CT: Bergin & Garvey.

Dunn, R., DeBello, T., Brennan, P., Krimsky, J., & Murrain, P. (1981). Learning style researchers define differences differently. *Educational Leadership, 38,* 372–375.

Dunn, R., & Dunn, K. (1972). *Practical approaches to individualizing instruction: Contracts and other effective teaching strategies.* Nyack, NY: Parker Publishing Company.

Dunn, R., & Dunn, K. (1978). *Teaching students through their individual learning styles: A practical approach.* Reston, VA: Prentice Hall.

Dunn, R., & Dunn, K. (1992). *Teaching elementary students through their individual learning styles: Practical approaches for grades 3–6.* Boston: Allyn & Bacon.

Dunn, R., & Dunn, K. (1993). *Teaching secondary students through their individual learning styles: Practical approaches for grades 7–12.* Boston: Allyn & Bacon.

Dunn, R., & Dunn, K. (1999). *The complete guide to the learning styles inservice system.* Boston: Allyn & Bacon.

Dunn, R., & Dunn, K. (2005). Thirty-five years of research on perceptual strengths. *The Clearing House, 78,* 273–276.

Dunn, R., & Dunn, K. (2008, March). Teaching to at-risk students' learning styles: Solutions based on international research. *Insights on Learning Disabilities: From Prevailing Theories to Validated Practices, 5*(1), 89–101.

Dunn, R., Dunn, K., & Perrin, J. (1994). *Teaching young children through their individual learning styles.* Boston: Allyn & Bacon.

Dunn, R., & Griggs, S. (1988). *Learning styles: Quiet revolution in American secondary schools.* Reston, VA: National Association of Secondary School Principals.

Dunn, R., & Griggs, S. A. (Eds.). (2003, 2004, 2007a). *Synthesis of the Dunn and Dunn learning-style model research: Who, what, when, where, and so what?* Jamaica, New York: St. John's University's Center for the Study of Learning and Teaching Styles.

Dunn, R., & Griggs, S. A. (Eds.). (2007b). *What if? Promising practices for improving education.* Lanham, MD: Rowman & Littlefield.

Dunn, R., Griggs, S. A., Milgram, R. M., & Price, G. E. (1997–1998). Learning styles of gifted adolescents in nine culturally-diverse nations. *National Forum of Applied Educational Research Journal, 10*(2), 3–18.

Dunn, R., & Missere, N. (2007). Learning In Vogue: Elements of Style (LIVES). www.learningstyles.net

Dunn, R., Rundle, S., & Burke, K. (2007). Elementary Learning Styles Assessment (ELSA). www.learningstyles.net.

Dunn, R., Thies, A. P., & Honigsfeld, A. (2001). *Synthesis of the Dunn and Dunn learning-style model research: Analysis from a neuropsychological perspective.* Jamaica, NY: St. John's University, Center for the Study of Learning and Teaching Styles.

Dunn, R., White, R. M., & Zenhausern, R. (1982). An investigation of responsible versus less responsible students. *Illinois School Research and Development, 19*(1), 19–24.

Ebel, R. L., (Ed.). (1969). *Encyclopaedia of educational research.* Toronto, Canada: Macmillan.

Edelman, S. (1998, Wednesday, June 10th). Showdown looms as two Rudys vow special-ed revamp. *New York Post*, p. 6.

Elliot, I. (1991, November/December). The reading place. *Teaching K–8, 21*(3), 30–34.

Favre, L. (2003). Impact of learning-style strategies on urban, poverty, minority students: Debunking the big city kid myth. In R. Dunn & S. A. Griggs (Eds.), *Synthesis of the Dunn and Dunn learning-style model research: Who, what, when, where, and so what?* (pp. 81–86). Jamaica, NY: St. John's University's Center for the Study of Learning and Teaching Styles.

Fine, D. (2002). Comparison between the learning styles of special and regular education high school students and the effects of responsive teaching on the short- and long-term achievement, attitudes, and behaviors of a subset of SPED adolescents (Doctoral dissertation, St. John's University, 2002). *Dissertation Abstracts International, 63*(01), 67A.

Fine, D. (2003). A sense of learning style. *Principal Leadership*, *4*(2), 55–59.

Gadwa, K., & Griggs, S. A. (1985). The school dropout: Implications for counselors. *School Counselor, 33*(1), 9–17.

Garrett, S. L. (1991). The effects of perceptual preference and motivation on vocabulary and attitude toward the learning task among selected high school students (Doctoral dissertation, University of La Verne, 1992). *Dissertation Abstracts International, 53*(02), 389A.

Geiser, W. F. (1999). Effects of learning-style responsive versus traditional study strategies on achievement, study, and attitudes of suburban eighth-grade mathematics students. *Research in Middle Level Education Quarterly, 22*(3), 19–41.

Greb, F. M. (1999). Learning-style preferences of fifth- through twelfth-grade students medically diagnosed with attention deficit/hyperactivity disorder (Doctoral dissertation, St. John's University, 1999). *Dissertation Abstracts International, 60*(03), 702A.

Gregorc, A. F. (1982). Learning style/brain research: Harbinger of an emerging psychology. In *Student learning styles and brain behavior* (pp. 3–10). Reston, VA: National Association of Secondary School Principals.

Gregorc, A. F. (1985). *Inside styles: Beyond the basics. A new definition for individuals.* Columbia, CT: Gregorc Associates.

Gremli, J. (1999). Effects of traditional versus contract activity package and programmed learning sequence instruction on the short- and long-term achievement and attitudes of seventh- and eight-grade general music students (Doctoral dissertation, St. John's University, 1999). *Dissertation Abstracts International,* 68. Recipient: International Network of Performing and Visual Arts Schools' 2003 Individual Research Award.

Gremli, J. (2001–2002). Learning sequenced instruction on the short- and long-term achievement of seventh- and eighth-grade general music students. *National Forum of Applied Educational Research Journal, 11*(2), 63–73.

Gremli, J. (2007). Impact of learning-style strategies on music. In Rita Dunn & Shirley A. Griggs (Eds.), *Synthesis of the Dunn and Dunn learning-style model research* (pp. 111–114). Jamaica, NY: St. John's University's Center for the Study of Learning and Teaching Styles.

Griggs, S. A. (1991). *Learning styles counseling*. Greensboro, NC: ERIC/CASS.

Guastello, E. F., & Burke, K. (1998–1999). Relationships between the consistency scores of an analytic vs. a global learning-style assessment for elementary- and middle-school urban students. In Dunn, R. & Griggs, S. A., (co-editors), *Learning Styles and Urban Education. The National Forum of Teacher Education Journal, 9*(1), 68–74.

Hill, J. (1971). *Personalized education programs utilizing cognitive style mapping*. Bloomfield Hills, MI: Oakland Community College.

Hlawaty, H. (2002). Comparative analysis of the learning styles of German versus other adolescents from diverse nations by age, gender, and academic achievement level (Doctoral dissertation, St. John's University, 2002). *Dissertation Abstracts International, 63*(06), 2112A.

Hlawaty, H. (2003, 2004, 2007). Learning styles of German adolescents. In R. Dunn & S. A. Griggs (Eds.). *Synthesis of the Dunn and Dunn learning-style model research: Who what, when, where, and so what?* (pp.141–144). Jamaica, NY: St. John's University's Center for the Study of Learning and Teaching Styles.

Hodges, H. (1985). An analysis of the relationships among preferences for a formal/informal design, one element of learning style, academic achievement, and attitudes of seventh and eighth grade students in remedial mathematics classes in a New York City junior high school (Doctoral dissertation, St. John's University, 1986). *Dissertation Abstracts International, 45*(12), 3585A. Recipient: Phi Delta Kappa National Finalist Award for Outstanding Doctoral Research, 1986.

Hong, E., Milgram, R. M., & Perkins, P. G. (1995). Homework style and homework behavior of Korean and American children. *Journal of Research and Development in Education, 28*, 197–207.

Hong, E., & Suh, B. (1995). An analysis of change in Korean-American and Korean students' learning styles. *Psychological Reports, 76*, 691–699.

Honigsfeld, A. (1999). Global warming: It's not cool! A model for creating multisensory instructional packages. *Science and Children, 36*(6), 46–51.

Honigsfeld, A. (2000). The learning styles of high-achieving and creative adolescents in Hungary. *Gifted and Talented International, 15*(1), 39–51.

Honigsfeld, A. (2001). A comparative analysis of the learning styles of adolescents from diverse nations by age, gender, academic achievement, and nationality (Doctoral dissertation, St. John's University, 2001). *Dissertation Abstracts International, 62*(03), 969A. Recipient: St. John's University's Outstanding Doctoral Research Award, 2001.

Honigsfeld, A. (2003a). Magyar tizenévesek tanulási stílusbeli preferenciái: a kor, a nem és a teljesítményszint hatásai. [Hungarian adolescents' learning style preferences by age, gender, and academic achievement.] *Magyar Pedagogia, 103*, 175–187.

Honigsfeld, A. (2003b, 2004, 2007). Learning styles of Hungarian adolescents. In R. Dunn & S. Griggs (Eds.), *Synthesis of the Dunn and Dunn learning styles model research: Who what, when, where, and so what?* (pp. 145–150). Jamaica, NY: St. John's University's Center for the Study of Learning and Teaching Styles.

Honigsfeld, A. & Cooper, A. (2003, 2004, 2007). Learning styles of New Zealand adolescents. In R. Dunn & S. Griggs (Eds.), *Synthesis of the Dunn and Dunn learning styles model research: Who what, when, where, and so what?* (pp. 151–154). Jamaica, NY: St. John's University's Center for the Study of Learning and Teaching Styles.

Honigsfeld, A., & Dunn, R. (2003). High school male and female learning-style similarities and differences in diverse nations. *Journal of Educational Research, 96,* 195–206.

Honigsfeld, A., & Gard, A. (2003). Learning styles of Swedish adolescents. In R. Dunn & S. A. Griggs (Eds.), *Synthesis of the Dunn and Dunn learning-style model research: Who, what, when, where, and so what?* (pp. 155–158). Jamaica, NY: St. John's University's Center for the Study of Learning and Teaching Styles.

Honigsfeld, A., & Lister, D. (2003). Learning styles of Bermudan students. In R. Dunn & S. A. Griggs (Eds.), *Synthesis of the Dunn and Dunn learning-style model research: Who, what, when, where, and so what?* (pp. 123–130). Jamaica, NY: St. John's University's Center for the Study of Learning and Teaching Styles.

Hunt, D. E. (1982). The practical value of learning style ideas. In *Student learning styles and brain behavior* (pp. 87–91). Reston, VA: National Association of Secondary School Principals.

Ingham, J. (1989). An experimental investigation of the relationships among learning style perceptual strength, instructional strategies, training achievement, and attitudes of corporate employees (Doctoral dissertation, St. John's University, 1990). *Dissertation Abstracts International, 51*(02), 380A. Recipient: American Society for Training and Development National Research Award (1990).

Ingham, J. M., Ponce Meza, R. M., & Price, G. (1998, November). A comparison of the learning style and creative talents of Mexican and American undergraduate engineering students. *Conference Proceedings, Frontiers in Education* (pp. 605–611). Tempe, AZ.

Ingham, J. M., & Price, G. E. (1993). The learning styles of gifted adolescents in the Philippines. In R. M. Milgram, R. Dunn, & G. E. Price, (Eds.), *Teaching and counseling gifted and talented adolescents: An international learning style perspective* (pp. 149–159). Westport, CT: Praeger.

Irvine, J. J., & York, D. E. (1995). Learning styles and culturally diverse students: A literature review. In J. A. Banks & C. A. Banks (Eds.), *Handbook of research on multicultural education.* New York: Macmillan.

Jarsonbeck, S. (1984). The effects of a right-brain mathematics curriculum on low-achieving, fourth-grade students (Doctoral dissertation, University of South Florida, 1984). *Dissertation Abstracts International, 45*(09), 2791A.

Karlova, U., Lekarska, F., & Kralove, H. (1994). Dotaznik stylu ucenti pro zaky zakladnich a strednich skol/LSI [The questionnaire of learning styles for pupils of basic and middle education schools]. *Psychologia-a-Patopsychologia-Dietat, 29*(3), 248–264.

Keefe, J. W. (1982). Assessing student learning styles: An overview. In *Student learning styles and brain behavior* (pp. 43–53). Reston, VA: National Association of Secondary School Principals.

Keefe, J. W., Letteri, C., Languis, M., & Dunn, R. (1985). *Learning style profile.* Reston, VA: NASSP.

Klavas, A. (1991). Implementation of the Dunn and Dunn learning style model in United States elementary schools: Factors which facilitated or impeded the process (Doctoral dissertation, St. John's University, 1997). *Dissertation Abstracts International, 58*(01), 88A.

Klavas, A., Dunn, R., Griggs, S. A., Gemake, J., Geisert, G., & Zenhausern, R. (1994). Factors that facilitated or impeded implementation of the Dunn and Dunn learning style model. *Illinois School Research and Development Journal, 31*(1), 19–23.

Kolb, D. A. (1976). *Learning style inventory.* Boston: McBer.

Lam-Phoon, S. (1986). A comparative study of the learning styles of southeast Asian and American Caucasian college students of two Seventh-day Adventist campuses (Doctoral dissertation, Andrews University, 1988). *Dissertation Abstracts International, 48*(09), 2234A.

Landy, N. (2005). Effects of tactual and kinesthetic instructional resources on Bermudian middle-school students' vocabulary achievement and attitudes (Doctoral dissertation, St. John's University, 2005). *Dissertation Abstracts International, 66*(09), 3239.

Lau, L. (1997). The perceptual preferences of a group of Malaysian kindergarten children and the effects of tactile and kinesthetic teaching methods on their learning of Bahasa Malaysia as a second language (Unpublished master's thesis, Massey University, New Zealand).

Lawrence, G. (1982). Personality structure and learning style: Use of the *Myers-Briggs Type Indicator*. In *Student learning styles and brain behavior* (pp. 92–105). Reston, VA: NASSP.

Lefkowitz, R. F. (2001). Effects of traditional versus learning-style presentation of course content in medical/legal issues in health care on the achievement and attitudes of college students (Doctoral dissertation, St. John's University). *Dissertation Abstracts International 61*(01), 69. Recipient: Phi Delta Kappa Award for Best Doctoral Research (2002).

Lefkowitz, R. F. (2006, Winter). Enhancement of achievement and attitudes toward learning of allied health students presented with traditional versus learning-style instruction on medical/legal issues of healthcare. *Perspectives in Health Information Management, 3*, 1.

Lefkowitz, R. F. (2007). Research on contract activity packages. In R. Dunn & S. A. Griggs (Eds.). *Synthesis of the Dunn and Dunn learning-style model research: Who, what, when, where, and so what?* (pp. 193–196). Jamaica, NY: St. John's University's Center for the Study of Learning and Teaching Styles.

Lenehan, M. C. (1994). Effects of learning-style knowledge on nursing majors' achievement, anxiety, anger, and curiosity (Doctoral dissertation, St. John's University, 1995). *Dissertation Abstracts International, 55*(11), 3426A.

Lenehan, M. C., Dunn, R., Ingham, J., Murray, W., & Signer, B. (1994). Learning style: Necessary know-how for academic success in college. *Journal of College Student Development, 35*, 461–465.

Leone, C. R. (2008). Parental support in the homework process: When students are drowning in homework, should parents be the life preserver? *Journal of the School Administrators of New York State, 37*, 6–11.

Levine, J. (2007). Comparative effects of alternative reading instructional approaches on the short- and long-term word recognition and attitude test scores of first-grade students (Doctoral dissertation, St. John's University, 2007).

Levy, J. (1982). Children think with whole brains: Myth and reality. In *Student learning styles and brain behavior* (pp. 173–184). Reston, VA: National Association of Secondary School Principals.

Li, T. C. (1989). The learning styles of the Filipino graduate students of the Evangelical seminaries in Metro Manila. (Unpublished doctoral dissertation, Asia Graduate School of Theology, Manila, Philippines).

Lister, D. (2004). Effects of traditional versus tactual and kinesthetic learning-style responsive instructional strategies on Bermudian learning-support sixth-grade students' social studies achievement and attitude test scores (Doctoral dissertation, St. John's University, 2004). *Dissertation Abstracts International, 65*(02), 466 (UMI No. 3123906).

Lo, H. M. (1994). A comparative study of learning styles of gifted, regular classroom, resource room/remedial program students in grades 3 to 5 in Taiwan, Republic of China (Doctoral dissertation, University of Missouri–Saint Louis, 1994). *Dissertation Abstracts International, 55*(06), 1471A.

Lovelace, M. K. (2005). A meta-analysis of experimental research based on the Dunn and Dunn learning-style model, 1980–2000. *Journal of Educational Research, 98*(3), 176–183. Recipient, Excellence in Research Award, School of Education, St. John's University.

Luria, A. R. (1973). *The working brain*. New York: Basic Books.

Marcus, L. (1977). A comparison of selected ninth-grade male and female students' learning styles. *The Journal, 6*(3), 27–28.

Mariash, L. J. (1983). Identification of learning styles existent among students attending school in selected Northeastern Manitoba communities (Unpublished master's thesis, University of Manitoba, Winnipeg, Canada).

Marino, J. (1993). Homework: A fresh approach to a perennial problem. *Momentum, 24*(1), 69–71.

Martini, M. (1986). An analysis of the relationships between and among computer assisted instruction, learning style perceptual preferences, attitudes, and the science achievement of seventh grade students in a suburban, New York school district (Doctoral dissertation, St. John's University, 1986). *Dissertation Abstracts International, 47*(03), 877A. Recipient: American Association of School Administrators (AASA) First Prize National Research, 1986.

McCarthy, B. (1990). *The 4MAT system: Teaching to learning styles with right/left mode techniques.* Barrington, IL: Excel.

Middle States Commission on Higher Education. (2003). *Student learning assessment: Options and resources.* Philadelphia, PA: Author.

Milgram, R. M., Dunn, R., & Price, G. E. (Eds.). (1993). *Teaching and counseling gifted and talented adolescents: An international learning style perspective.* Westport, CT: Praeger.

Miller, J., Ostrow, S., Dunn, R., Beasley, M., Geisert, G., & Nelson, B. (2000–2001). Effects of traditional versus learning-style presentation of course content in ultrasound and anatomy on the achievement and attitudes of allied-health college students. *National Forum of Applied Educational Research Journal, 13*(1), 50–62.

Ming, C. (2004). Effects of programmed learning sequenced versus traditional instruction on the achievement and attitudes of Bermudian seventh graders in social studies and the comparison of two learning-style identification instruments' interpretations (Doctoral dissertation, St. John's University, 2004). *Dissertation Abstracts International 66*(03), 850A.

Ming, C. S. (2007). Research on programmed learning sequences. In R. Dunn & S. A. Griggs (Eds.), *Synthesis of the Dunn and Dunn learning-style model research: Who, what, when, where, and so what?* (pp. 203–208). Jamaica, NY: St. John's University's Center for the Study of Learning and Teaching Styles.

Ming, C., & Ansalone, G. (2006). Programming students for academic success: The PLS alternative to traditional tracking. *Academic Research Quarterly, 29*(3), 3–10.

Minotti, J. L. (2002). Effect of learning-style based homework prescriptions on the achievement and attitudes of middle-school students. (Doctoral dissertation, St. John's University, 2002). *Dissertation Abstracts International*, 63(04), 1248A.

Mitchell, D., Dunn, R., Klavas, A., Lynch, V., Montgomery, N., & Murray, W. (2002). Effects of traditional versus tactual/kinesthetic instruction on junior-high school learning-disabled students. *Academic Exchange Quarterly, 6*(3), 115–122.

Mochizuki, K. (1995). *Baseball saved us.* New York: Lee and Low Books.

Monsour, S. E. M. (1991). The relationship between a prescribed homework program considering learning style preferences and the math achievement of eighth-grade students (Doctoral dissertation, The University of Southern Mississippi, 1991). *Dissertation Abstracts International, 52*(06), 1630A.

Murray-Harvey, R. (1994). Learning styles and approaches to learning: Distinguishing between concepts and instruments. *British Journal of Educational Psychology, 64*, 373–388.

Neely, R., & Alm, D. (1992). Meeting individual needs: A learning styles success story. *The Clearing House, 66*, 109–113.

Neely, R., & Alm, D. (1993). Empowering students with style. *Principal, 72*(4), 32–35.

Nelson, B. J. (1991). An investigation of the impact of learning style factors on college students' retention and achievement (Doctoral dissertation, St. John's University, 1991). *Dissertation Abstracts International, 53*(09), 3121A.

Nelson, B., Dunn, R., Griggs, S. A., Primavera, L., Fitzpatrick, M., Bacilious, Z., et al., (1993). Effects of learning style intervention on students' retention and achievement. *Journal of College Student Development, 34*, 364–369.

Nganwa-Bagumah, M., & Mwamwenda, T. S. (1991). Effects on reading comprehension tests of matching and mismatching students' design preferences. *Perceptual and Motor Skills, 72*, 947–951.

Oberer, J. (1999). Practical application of Thies' philosophical and theoretical interpretation of the biological basis of learning style and brain behavior and their effects on the academic achievement, attitudes, and behaviors of fourth-grade students in a suburban school district (Doctoral dissertation, St. John's University, 2000). *Dissertation Abstracts International, 48*(02), 283A.

Oberer, J. J. (2003). Effects of learning-style teaching on elementary students' behaviors, achievement, and attitudes. *Academic Exchange Quarterly,* 7(1), 193–199.

O'Connell, D. M. (1999). *Comparative values scale.* Jamaica, NY: St. John's University.

O'Connell, D. (2000). Effects of traditional instruction versus teacher-constructed and student-constructed instructional resources on the short- and long-term achievement and attitudes of tenth-grade science students (Doctoral dissertation, St. John's University, 2000). *Dissertation Abstracts International, 61*(04), 1345A.

Ogden, D. (1989). Student application of learning styles and modality preferences as shown in achievement and attitude (Doctoral dissertation, Northern Arizona University). *Dissertation Abstracts International, 51*(05)A, 1496.

Orazio, P. (1999). Effect of matching and mismatching learning style global and traditional analytic instructional resources on the achievement and attitudes of seventh-grade mathematics students (Doctoral dissertation, St. John's University, 1999). *Dissertation Abstracts International, 59*(12), 4386A.

Orden, M. V. (2004). Perceptual strengths and hemispheric preferences of St. Mary's University's education students and faculty, school year 2003–2004: A co-relational study. *Saint Mary's University Research Journal, 6,* 1–54. Retrieved June 1, 2008, from http://research.smu.edu.ph/images/stories/pdf/smurj6iya-newest.pdf.

Orden, M. V., & Querol, C. B. (2005). Engineering and architecture teachers' and students' hemispheric preferences and perceptual strengths as related to selected personal, family, and academic variables. *St. Mary's University's Research Journal, 7,* 169–218.

Orden, M. V., & Ramos, B. (2005). Perceptual strengths of college freshmen of Saint Mary's University and their response to physiological, psychological, sociological, emotional, and environmental stimuli: A comparative and correlational analysis. *St. Mary's University's Research Journal, 7*, 109–145. Retrieved June 1, 2008, from http://research.smu.edu.ph/images/stories/pdf/rjvol7ordenramosrev.pdf.

Orsak, L. (1990). Learning styles versus the Rip Van Winkle syndrome. *Educational Leadership, 48*(2), 19–20.

Pengiran-Jadid, P. R. (1998). Analysis of the learning styles, gender, and creativity of Bruneian performing and non-performing primary and elite and regular secondary school students and their teachers' teaching styles (Doctoral dissertation, St. John's University, 1998). *Dissertation Abstracts International, 59*(06), 1893A.

Pengiran-Jadid, R. (2003, 2004, 2007). Learning styles of Bruneian adolescents. In R. Dunn & S. A. Griggs (Eds.), *Synthesis of the Dunn and Dunn learning-style model research* (pp. 135–141). Jamaica, NY: St. John's University's Center for the Study of Learning and Teaching Styles.

Perna, M. (2007). Effects of Total Physical Response Storytelling versus traditional, versus initial instruction with primary-, reinforced by secondary-perceptual strengths on the vocabulary- and grammar-Italian-language-achievement test scores, and the attitudes of ninth and tenth graders. Ed.D. dissertation, St. John's University (New York), United States—New York. Retrieved September 21, 2008, from Dissertations & Theses: Full Text database. (Publication No. AAT 3279261).

Perrin, J. (1990). The learning styles project for potential dropouts. *Educational Leadership, 48*(2), 23–24.

Pizzo, J. (1981). An investigation of the relationship between selected acoustic environments and sound, an element of learning style, as they affect sixth-grade students' reading achievement and attitudes (Doctoral dissertation, St. John's University, 1981). *Dissertation Abstracts International, 42*(06), 2475A. Recipient: Association for Supervision and Curriculum Development First Alternate National Recognition for Best Doctoral Research in Curriculum, 1981.

Pizzo, J., Dunn, R., & Dunn, K. (1990). A sound approach to reading: Responding to students' learning styles. *Journal of Reading, Writing, and Learning Disability,* 6, 307–314.

Prelutsky, J. (1983). Me I am. In *The Random House book of poetry for children.* New York: Random House.

Price, G. E. (1980). Which learning style elements are stable and which tend to change over time? *Learning Styles Network Newsletter, 1*(3), 1.

Quinn, R. (1993). The New York State compact for learning and learning styles. *Learning Styles Network Newsletter, 15*(1), 1–2.

Quinn, R. (1999). *The Bridge to Learning.* Videotape describing Buffalo's Learning Style Program. Buffalo, NY: Buffalo City Schools under a New York State Education Department Grant. Available from St. John's University's Center for the Study of Learning and Teaching Styles.

Ramirez, A. I. (1982). Modality and field dependence-independence: Learning style components and their relationship to mathematics achievement in the elementary school (Doctoral dissertation, The Florida State University, 1982). *Dissertation Abstracts International, 43*(03), 666A.

Ramirez, M., & Castaneda, A. (1974). *Cultural democracy, bicognitive development, and education.* New York: Academic Press.

Raupers, P. M. (1999). Effects of accommodating perceptual learning-style preferences on long term retention and attitudes toward technology of elementary and secondary teachers in professional development training (Doctoral dissertation, St. John's University, 1999). *Dissertation Abstracts International, 59*(11), 4031A.

Raviotta, C. F. (1989). A study of the relationship between knowledge of individual learning style and its effect on academic achievement and study orientation in high school mathematics students (Doctoral dissertation, University of New Orleans, 1989). *Dissertation Abstracts International, 50*(05), 1204A.

Reese, V., & Dunn, R. (2007–2008). Learning-style preferences of a diverse freshman population in a large, private metropolitan university by gender and GPA. *Journal of College Student Retention, Research, Theory & Practice, 9*(1), 95–112.

Restak, R. M. (1979). The other difference between boys and girls. In *Student learning styles: Diagnosing and prescribing programs* (pp. 75–80). Reston, VA: National Association of Secondary School Principals.

Roberts, O. A. (1984). An investigation of the relationship between learning style and temperament of senior high students in the Bahamas and Jamaica (Master's thesis, Andrews University, 1984). *Masters Abstracts International,* 2303.

Roberts, S. (2004–2005). Effects of traditional, programmed learning sequenced, and contract activity packaged instruction on sixth-grade students' achievement and attitudes. *National Forum of Applied Educational Research Journal, 18*(1), 50–74.

Sagan, L. (2002). Middle-school students' recommendations of environmental and instructional change based on their analyses of individual learning-style inventories (Doctoral dissertation, St. John's University 2002). *Dissertation Abstracts International, 66*(09), 3260A.

Schmeck, R. R. (1977). *Inventory of Learning Processes.* Carbondale, IL: Department of Psychology, Southern Illinois University.

Scricca, D. B. (2007). Administrative guidelines for staff development based on secondary-school teachers' learning styles: Impact on classroom implementation and teachers' attitudes (Doctoral dissertation, St. John's University).

Sheehan, K. (2008). Helping children discover the big ideas. *Social Science Docket, 8*(1), 2–3.

Shemer, M. (1995). *Learning style, homework style and creative thinking in adolescents* (Unpublished master's thesis, Tel Aviv University, Israel).

Simplicio, J. S. C. (2007). *Educating the 21st century student.* Bloomington, IN: AuthorHouse.

Sinatra, R., Sazo de Mendez, E., & Price, G. E. (1993). The learning styles and creative performance accomplishments of adolescents in Guatemala. In R. M. Milgram, R. Dunn, & G. E. Price (Eds.), *Teaching and counseling gifted and talented adolescents: An international learning style perspective* (pp. 161–173). Westport, CT: Praeger.

Soliman, A. S. (1993). The learning styles of adolescents in Egypt. In R. M. Milgram, R. Dunn, & G. E. Price (Eds.), *Teaching and counseling gifted and talented adolescents: An international learning style perspective* (pp. 211–218). Westport, CT: Praeger.

Spiridakis, J. (1993). The learning styles of adolescents in Greece. In R. M. Milgram, R. Dunn, & G. E. Price (Eds.), *Teaching and counseling gifted and talented adolescents: An international learning style perspective* (pp. 219–227). Westport, CT: Praeger.

Stone, P. (1992). How we turned around a problem school. *Principal, 71*(2), 34–36.

Suh, B., & Price, G. E. (1993). The learning styles of gifted adolescents in Korea. In R. M. Milgram, R. Dunn, & G. E. Price (Eds.), *Teaching and counseling gifted and talented adolescents: An international learning style perspective* (pp. 174–185). Westport, CT: Praeger.

Tanenbaum, R. (1982). An investigation of the relationship(s) between selected instructional techniques and identified field dependent and field independent cognitive styles as evidenced among high school students enrolled in studies of nutrition (Doctoral dissertation, St. John's University, 1982). *Dissertation Abstracts International, 43*(01), 68A.

Taylor, R. G. (1999). Effects of learning-style responsive versus traditional staff development on the knowledge and attitudes of urban and suburban elementary school teachers (Doctoral dissertation, St. John's University, 1999). *Dissertation Abstracts International, 60*(04), 1089A.

Tendy, S. M., & Geiser, W. F. (1998–1999). The search for style: It all depends on where you look. *National Forum of Teacher Education Journal, 9*(1), 3–15.

Thies, A. P. (1979). A brain-behavior analysis of learning styles. In *Student learning styles: Diagnosing and prescribing programs* (pp. 55–61). Reston, VA: National Association of Secondary School Principals.

Thies, A. P. (1999–2000). The neuropsychology of learning styles. *National Forum of Applied Educational Research Journal, 13*(1), 50–62.

Trautman, P. (1979). An investigation of the relationship between selected instructional techniques and identified cognitive style (Doctoral dissertation, St. John's University, 1979). *Dissertation Abstracts International, 40*(03), 1428A.

Tully, D. (2004). Effects of programmed learning sequenced and tactual and kinesthetic instructional materials on the mathematics fractions test scores of sixth graders in a Bermuda middle school (Doctoral dissertation, St. John's University, 2004). *Dissertation Abstracts International*, *65*(06), 2050A.

Tully, D., Dunn, R., & Hlawaty, H. (October, 2006). Effects of programmed learning sequences on the mathematics test scores of Bermudian middle-school students. *Research in Middle-Level Education Online, 30*(2), 1–11.

Turner, N. D. (1992). A comparative study of the effects of learning style prescriptions and/or modality-based instruction on the spelling achievement of fifth-grade students (Doctoral dissertation, Andrews University, 1992). *Dissertation Abstracts International, 53*(04), 1051A.

Ulubabova, T. (2003, 2004, 2007). Learning styles of Russian adolescents. In R. Dunn & S. A. Griggs, (Eds.), *Synthesis of the Dunn and Dunn learning-style model research: Who, what, when, where, and so what?* (pp. 159–164). Jamaica, NY: St. John's University's Center for the Study of Learning and Teaching Styles.

Urbschat, K. S. (1977). A study of preferred learning modes and their relationship to the amount of recall of CVC trigrams (Doctoral dissertation, Wayne State University, 1977). *Dissertation Abstracts International, 38*(05), 2536A.

Van Wynen, E. (1999). The relationships between selected learning-style elements and the achievement and attitudes of older adults following wellness sessions using different instructional methodologies (Doctoral dissertation, St. John's University, 1999). *Dissertation Abstract International*, *62*(05), 1740A. Recipient:

Sigma Theta Tau International Honor Society of Nursing for best doctoral proposal, 1998.

Van Wynen, E. (2001). A key to successful aging: Learning-style patterns of older adults. *Journal of Erotological Nursing, 29*(9), 6–15.

Vazquez, A. W. (1985). Description of learning styles of high-risk adult students taking evening courses in urban community colleges in Puerto Rico (Doctoral dissertation, The Union for Experimenting Colleges and Universities, 1986). *Dissertation Abstracts International, 47*(04), 1157A.

Wechsler, S. (1993). The learning styles of creative adolescents in Brazil. In R. M. Milgram, R. Dunn, & G. E. Price (Eds.), *Teaching and counseling gifted and talented adolescents: An international learning style perspective* (pp. 197–209). Westport, CT: Praeger.

Wheeler, R. (1983). An investigation of the degree of academic achievement evidenced when second grade, learning disabled students' perceptual preferences are matched and mismatched with complementary sensory approaches to beginning reading instruction (Doctoral dissertation, St. John's University, 1984). *Dissertation Abstracts International, 44*(07), 2039A.

White, M. E. (1996). Effects of homework prescriptions based upon individual learning-style preferences on the achievement and attitude toward mathematics of sixth-grade students (Doctoral dissertation, University of Alabama at Birmingham, 1997). *Dissertation Abstracts International, 57*(08), 3384.

Wood, M. (2002). Effects of individualized plans independent of, and supplemented by, learning-style profiles on the mathematics achievement and attitudes of special education students in grades three through six. (Doctoral dissertation, St. John's University, 2002). *Dissertation Abstracts International*, 63(04), 1304A.

Yeap, L. L. (1987). Learning styles of Singapore secondary two students (Doctoral dissertation, University of Pittsburgh, 1987). *Dissertation Abstracts International, 49*(07), 1744A.

Zenhausern, R. (1982). Education and the left hemisphere. In *Student learning styles and brain behavior* (pp. 192–195). Reston, VA: National Association of Secondary School Principals.

About the Authors

Rita Dunn joined the faculty of St. John's University in 1970; designed its Instructional Leadership doctoral program in 1972; has served as its coordinator since 1979; became the first woman full professor in the School of Education in 1976; and, since 1979, has served as director of the Center for the Study of Learning and Teaching Styles. She also served as Chair of the Division of Administrative and Instructional Leadership.

Dr. Dunn received St. John's University's First Outstanding Faculty Achievement Gold Medal and its First Award for Excellence in Graduate Teaching. To date, she has mentored 157 doctoral students, of which 32 have won national and international recognition for the quality of their research. She was the recipient of St. John's University's Faculty Merit Award every year between 1989 and 2000, and again in 2002 (when it was discontinued). Dr. Dunn is the author of 31 books and more than 500 published book chapters, monographs, and articles. She was a New York University Founder's Day Honors Scholar in 1967 and received NYU's Research Scholarship Award in 1966. She also was elected to the Hunter College Hall of Fame.

The National Association of Elementary School Principals designated her "Educator of the Year" at its national convention in San Francisco in 1988, the Association for Supervision and Curriculum Development named her "Outstanding Consultant of the Year" in 1982, St. John's University's Phi Delta Kappa chapter awarded her the same title in 1990, and she was cited, "Distinguished Lecturer of the Year" by the American Association of School Administrators at its National Convention in New Orleans in 1985.

Andrea Honigsfeld completed the doctorate in Instructional Leadership at St. John's University in 2001 and was the recipient of several awards, including the Outstanding Doctoral Research Award, Certificate of Academic

Excellence, and the Certificate of Merit from the School of Education and Human Services. She is associate professor and associate dean in the Division of Education at Molloy College in Rockville Centre, New York.

In fall 2002, the Fulbright Scholarship that she was awarded took her to Iceland to collaborate with a pioneering group of professors in the graduate division of the Iceland University of Education to develop a new certificate program in multicultural education. Dr. Honigsfeld has published on topics such as learning styles, TESOL, and multicultural education. In 2007, she was honored with the New York State TESOL Outstanding Teacher Award.

Robin Boyle is professor of legal writing and coordinator of the Academic Support Program at St. John's University School of Law. Since 1994 when Professor Boyle began teaching at the law school, she has been conducting research inside and outside of her classroom using the Dunn and Dunn Learning-Style Model. Her articles, book chapters, and essays appear in numerous legal and other academic publications. She presents frequently at regional, national, and international conferences on the topics of learning styles and teaching.

Previous Books by the Authors

PREVIOUS BOOKS BY RITA DUNN

Dunn, R., & Blake, B. E. (Eds.). (2008). *Teaching every child to read: Innovative and practical strategies for K–8 educators.* Lanham, MD: Rowman & Littlefield Education.

Dunn, R., & Griggs, S. A. (2007). *What if . . . ? A practical guide to improving education.* Lanham, MD: Rowman & Littlefield Education.

Milgram, R. M., Dunn, R., & Price, G. E. (2006). *Counseling gifted children: A guide for teachers, counselors, and parents.* Greenwood Publishing Group, Chinese Edition, 285 pp.

Rundle, S., Honigsfeld, A., & Dunn, R. (2005). *Educators' guide to building excellence.* Darien, CT: Performance Concepts.

Dunn, R., & Griggs, S. A. (2003, 2004). *Synthesis of the Dunn and Dunn learning-style model research: Who, what, when, where, and so what?* New York: St. John's University's Center for the Study of Learning and Teaching Styles.

Dunn, R. (2001). *Teaching young adults to teach themselves.* Sweden: Brain Books.

Dunn, R., & Griggs, S. A. (Eds.). (2000). *Practical approaches to using learning styles in higher education.* Westport, CT: Bergin & Garvey.

Dunn, R., & DeBello, T. C. (Eds.). (1999) *Improved test scores, attitudes, and behaviors in America's schools: Supervisors' success stories.* Westport, CT: Bergin & Garvey.

Dunn, R., & Dunn K. (1999). *The complete guide to the learning styles in-service system.* Boston: Allyn & Bacon.

Dunn, R., & Dunn, K. (Eds.). (1998). *Practical approaches to individualizing staff development for adults.* Westport, CT: Greenwood.

Dunn, R., & Griggs, S. A. (1998). *Learning styles and the nursing profession.* New York: National League of Nursing.

Dunn, R. (1996). *How to implement and supervise a learning style program.* Alexandria, VA: Association for Supervision and Curriculum Development.

Dunn, R. (1996). *Everything you need to successfully implement a learning styles instructional program: Materials and methods.* New Wilmington, PA: Association for the Advancement of International Education.

Dunn, R., & Griggs, S. A. (1995). *Multiculturalism and learning styles: Teaching and counseling adolescents.* Westport, CT: Greenwood.

Dunn, R. (1995). *Educating diverse learners: Strategies for improving current class-room practices.* Bloomington, IN: Phi Delta Kappa.

Dunn, R., & Dunn, K., & Perin, J. (1994). *Teaching young children through their individual learning styles.* Boston: Allyn & Bacon.

Milgram, R. M., Dunn, R., & Price, G. E. (Eds.). (1993). *Teaching and counseling gifted and talented adolescents: An international learning styles perspective.* Westport, CT: Praeger.

Dunn, R., Dunn, K., & Treffinger, D. (1992). *Bringing out the giftedness in every child: A guide for parents.* New York: John Wiley & Sons.

Dunn, R., & Dunn, K. (1993). *Teaching secondary students through their individual learning styles.* Boston: Allyn & Bacon, Inc.

Dunn, R., & Dunn, K. (1992). *Teaching elementary students through their individual learning styles.* Boston: Allyn & Bacon, Inc.

Dunn, R., & Dunn, K. (1992). *Teaching primary students through their individual learning styles.* Boston: Allyn & Bacon, Inc.

Dunn, R. (1991). *Hands-on approaches to learning styles: A practical guide to successful schooling.* New Wilmington, PA: The Association for the Advancement of International Education, 63 pp.

Dunn, R., & Griggs, S. A. (1988). *Learning styles: Quiet revolution in American secondary schools.* Reston, VA: National Association of Secondary School Principals.

Carbo, M., Dunn, R., & Dunn K. (1986). *Teaching students to read through their individual learning styles.* Englewood Cliffs, NJ: Prentice Hall.

Dunn, R., & Dunn, K. (1983). *Situational leadership for principals: The school administrator in action.* Englewood Cliffs, NJ: Prentice-Hall.

Dunn, R., & Dunn, K. (1978). *Teaching students through their individual learning styles: A practical approach.* Reston, VA: Reston Publishing Company–a Prentice Hall Division.

Dunn, R., & Dunn, K. (1977). *How to raise independent and professionally successful daughters.* Englewood Cliffs, NJ: Prentice Hall.

Dunn, R., & Dunn, K. (1977). *Administrator's guide to new programs for faculty management and evaluation.* Nyack, NY: Parker Publishing Company, a Prentice Hall Division.

Dunn, R., & Dunn, K. (1975). *Educator's self-teaching guide to individualizing instructional programs.* Nyack, NY: Parker Publishing Company, a Prentice Hall Division.

Dunn, R., & Dunn, K. (1972). *Practical approaches to individualizing instruction: Contracts and other effective teaching strategies.* Nyack, NY: Parker Publishing Company, a Prentice Hall Division.

PREVIOUS BOOKS BY ANDREA HONIGSFELD

Honigsfeld, A. (1993). Hungarolingua Video Munkafüzet 2 [Video workbook for intermediate learners of Hungarian]. Debrecen, Hungary: Kossuth Lajos University Press.

Rundle, S., Honigsfeld, A., & Dunn, R. (2002). *An educator's guide to the learning individual.* Rochester, NY: Performance Concepts International.

La Belle Dillon, J., Honigsfeld, A., Rundle, S. M., & Watson, W. E. (2005). *Building excellence through students: Freshman seminar textbook.* Rochester, NY: Performance Concepts International.